SPIRITS
OF THE COAST

SPIRITS

OF THE COAST

ORCAS IN SCIENCE, ART AND HISTORY

EDITED BY **MARTHA BLACK, LORNE HAMMOND** AND **GAVIN HANKE**, WITH **NIKKI SANCHEZ**

ROYAL **BC** MUSEUM
VICTORIA, CANADA

Spirits of the Coast: Orcas in Science, Art and History

Essays by Nikki Sanchez, Martha Black, Lorne Hammond and Gavin Hanke © the Royal BC Museum, 2020. All other essays, photographs and illustrations © the creators as credited, 2020 unless otherwise noted.

Published by the Royal BC Museum, 675 Belleville Street, Victoria, British Columbia, V8W 9W2, Canada.

The Royal BC Museum is located on the traditional territories of the Lekwungen (Songhees and Xwsepsum Nations). We extend our appreciation for the opportunity to live and learn on this territory.

Design by Lara Minja, Lime Design Inc.
Index by Catherine Plear

Title spread, pp. ii–iii: *Protection* by Andy Everson, © 2008. See p. 191 for artist's statement.

Contents, pp. vi–vii: Viewing T74, a Bigg's orca, from a canoe carved from a Meares Island tree. Tofino Harbour, Clayoquot Sound. Kyler Vos photo.

Artwork, p. viii: Aerial photograph of a group of Southern Resident killer whales from L pod, 2017. Image collected non-invasively during scientific research using an octocopter drone at an altitude of over 100 feet above the whales, with research authorized by NMFS permit 19091. Photo by John Durban (NOAA) and Holly Fearnbach (SR3).

Library and Archives Canada Cataloguing in Publication

Title: Spirits of the coast : orcas in science, art and history / edited by Martha Black, Lorne Hammond and Gavin Hanke, with Nikki Sanchez.

Names: Black, Martha, editor. | Hammond, Lorne, 1955– editor. | Hanke, Gavin, 1967– editor. | Sanchez, Nikki, 1986– editor. | Royal British Columbia Museum, publisher.

Description: Includes bibliographical references and index. | Text in English with some text in Haida and Nootka.

Identifiers: Canadiana (print) 20200175025 | Canadiana (ebook) 20200175033 | ISBN 9780772677686

(hardcover) | ISBN 9780772677709 (EPUB) | ISBN 9780772677716 (Kindle) | ISBN 9780772677693 (PDF)

Subjects: LCSH: Killer whale.

Classification: LCC QL737.C432 S65 2020 | DDC 599.53/6—dc23

10 9 8 7 6 5 4 3 2 1

Printed and bound in Canada by Friesens.

To all the future generations of the Salish Sea.
From the gooseneck barnacles in the intertidal zone to the bald eagles who watch from above, and every creature in between. May you always know the power, grace and magnificence of your Resident orca population.

CONTENTS

ARTWORK

FOREWORD

Jack Lohman, CBE
CEO, ROYAL BC MUSEUM

In August 2019, a 15-year-old Bigg's orca was spotted in Victoria's Inner Harbour, steps from the Royal BC Museum. The sighting was rare enough that media rushed to get a glimpse, as did tourists and locals—many capturing the orca's voyage on mobile phones from the shoreline, from water taxis plying the harbour and from nearby office buildings.

The reason for the orca's visit was unclear. Biologists speculate that it may have been hunting for food, but also that it may simply have been curious, exploring the human-dredged harbour as it might any natural inlet or fjord.

Indigenous people in what is now called British Columbia have always thought of orcas as relatives. This was not often the case for settler, secular empiricists like myself, whose view of orcas has changed substantially in recent decades. Those who once called them "killers" now see them as near-kin. We now accept a biologist's hypothesis of *curiosity* as a motivating factor for what seems to

us non-orcas to be anomalous behaviour. This remarkable book takes us beneath the ocean to inhabit the world of the orca.

It also takes us among cultural viewpoints, featuring perspectives from Indigenous people, scientists and activists in British Columbia and around the world. The book includes works by contributors whose roots reach from the Hawai'ian Islands to the fjords of Haida Gwaii, from urban Africa to the coast of New Zealand, reflecting the diversity of relationships and perspectives humans around the world have about not only orcas, but animal rights, the fate of our oceans and human kinship with the rest of the tree of life. The powerful, personal introduction by Indigenous writer Nikki Sanchez, the book's mastermind, is as bracing and wakening as a headlong dive into the deep green saltchuck.

Looking beneath the surface is what museums do. Whether that surface is the rippling skin of the ocean or the veneer of historical "truth," museums like to slip between one world and another to explore a very different reality.

RAINY PASSAGE **APRIL BENCZE**

An orca travels through the territorial waters of the Haíɫzaqv Nation with their familial pod, 2015.

Spirits of the Coast is a superb contextual companion to the Royal BC Museum's 2020 feature exhibition *Orcas: Our Shared Future*, but it can be enjoyed on its own. The chapters are the product of immense and diverse talent, with contributions from literary, scientific and cultural luminaries.

I am gratified that this Royal BC Museum publication will be your anchor in a cultural, scientific and historical voyage, pulling you with gravity and grace into the orca's world. When you resurface, I trust it will be with a new sense of wonder and appreciation for the orca, and a better understanding of our complex relationship with it.

INTRODUCTION

Nikki Sanchez

Two years ago, my mother had a dream. In it, the Southern Resident orcas came to her and communicated that they urgently needed human help. They took her underwater and showed her their world; she swam with them and saw first-hand the conditions that were causing them to suffer, the reasons they were dying. They took her to the places their descendants had travelled and hunted for millennia, around the islands, straits, estuaries and secret coves. In the dream she felt the sonic assault of the marine tankers, the panic of the dwindling chinook, the chaotic accumulation of ocean debris and the contamination of the waters.

Our family was no stranger to grief at the time: the previous year, my mother's husband had struggled to get through each day as his body was overtaken by a terminal illness. Maybe the dream was a manifestation of her grief, or maybe it was a reflection of the depth of her connection to our coastal orca kin. Either way, it moved her into action. Together

with her intertidal friends and me, we put out a call to anyone concerned about the wellbeing of the local Resident orcas to come together. Within a few weeks, 30 of us gathered at an art studio on Salt Spring Island. Our group, made up primarily of women 20 to 80 years of age, spent the day talking about our concerns for the orcas and what we could do for them. The one thing everyone shared in common was their love for these whales and the awe they evoked in us.

We decided that it would be love and awe that guided our movement. We wanted to harness love rather than fear as the catalyst to call others into action, and in the end, we decided art would be our vehicle. We named the group Orca Soundings and set out to create an artistic representation of the orcas in the Salish Sea Resident population. I laugh to myself when I think of our early attempts to construct these models: though they were not quite lifesize, we wanted them to be big enough to draw attention, light enough to carry at public events, and made from natural materials so that their creation wouldn't cause further environmental harm. I have vivid memories of bushwhacking along the rocky coast of Beaver Point to harvest gorse (*Ulex europaeus*), the first material we attempted to build our orcas out of. By the time we emerged from the deep underbrush, I was covered in prickles and entirely discouraged.

In the end, an environmental artist from Salt Spring Island created a model template for our orcas out of plywood and non-toxic paint. Then there were grandmother orca puppets made of willow and fabric, and a large number of elegant dorsal fins—one for each member of the Southern Resident orca population. Each orca was matched with a human advocate, someone who would carry their whale to marches, Earth Day celebrations and the like and tell the story of their individual orca with the hope of educating about the reasons their survival was threatened. At the time we created these models, the population of the Southern Resident orcas was 80.

At the time of this writing, that number has dropped to 73. I have no way of knowing how many will remain when you are reading this, but it is my profound hope—a hope that I know is shared by all who contributed to this anthology—that this work will be not a eulogy, but rather a

celebration, a unification of many through our shared love to take action to ensure this orca population, analogous to all the marine species of our world, not only survives, but thrives.

However, I do not expect anyone to take action, make sacrifices, or fight for something they don't love. So that is what this book is: an invitation to fall in love, in awe, with these incredible marine mammals, so that we can come together to protect them. And as you will learn in the pages to come, the survival of orcas—apex predators, just as humans are—is not distinct from our own.

This anthology brings together orca experts of every category, from neuroscientists-turned-activists to emerging Indigenous writers and artists who carry forward the sacred knowledge systems of their ancestors. The collection of voices spans ancient covenants of orca/human treaty, stories of the past, detailed legacies of the evolution of orca imagery in our collective imagination, and the most recent research regarding orca behaviour, communication and survival.

This anthology is divided into three sections: Connection, Captivity and Consciousness. Connection spans time and culture, from pre-colonial accounts of human/orca interdependence, governance and treaty with coastal peoples to the forging of human/orca relationships

THE INCLUSION AND SELECTION OF ART WAS REGARDED WITH THE SAME CARE AND CONSIDERATION AS WERE THE WRITTEN PIECES—NOT ART FOR ADORNMENT, BUT ART AS STORIES, REFLECTIONS, INVITATIONS TO WONDER AND WITH AN IMPERATIVE MESSAGE IN AND OF ITSELF.

from within a settler worldview through the lenses of science, literature, music and media. The Captivity section tells the stories of an era of human/orca relations that were dictated by the flawed understanding of orcas as killers, commodities and insentient monsters from personal, scientific and cumulative perspectives. This section reveals the impacts of this worldview on both human and orca populations. The last section of the book, Consciousness, offers a window into a plethora of alternate imaginings of what a reciprocal path forward could look like.

In the formation of this book, we cast a broad net, with the intention of creating a collection of orca content as diverse as orcas' impacts on our human experience have been, and equally powerful and poignant. What you will discover in the pages to come is a compilation of perspectives that together create a mosaic of how orcas have come to be known and understood in the current human zeitgeist. The work includes scientific

studies, cultural records, oral histories, poetry, and visions of the past and future encapsulated through words, art and images. The inclusion and selection of art was regarded with the same care and consideration as were the written pieces— not art for adornment, but art as stories, reflections, invitations to wonder and with an imperative message in and of itself. The decision to make art a central element of this work was made because we knew that like orca forms of communication, not all knowledge can be shared through words. There has not been a single day on this project, which has brought together such a distinguished array of minds and imaginations, when I have not sat humbled by reverence—for the brilliant minds who have shared their passionate perspectives in this collection, but also for the orcas themselves, who have ignited the passion that is exhibited here.

As is repeatedly conveyed in the pages to come, despite the current neoliberal paradigm, we are not separate from our world. Nor can we remove ourselves from it in order to examine it. And thus, this anthology does not attempt to present itself as anything other than exactly what it is: a collection of human perspectives, reflections, experiences and testaments regarding our knowledge of and connection to the orca whale. The other side of this story remains to be told by the orcas themselves.

To reiterate what I stated above, because my elders have always taught me that when something is very important we must repeat it many times, it is my profound hope that this book will not be a eulogy, but a celebration, a call to action, an invitation to fall in love with our magnificent kin: the orca whales. May this book be a testament of love, accountability and commitment to standing up to ensuring that they, and we, have a sustainable path forward, a future worth striving for. May the generations to come tell the story not of our failure, but of our triumph that against many odds, we found a path to collective survival.

And with these words, I invite you to be a witness, a living record, a piece of this collective triumph of survival with our relatives, the orcas.

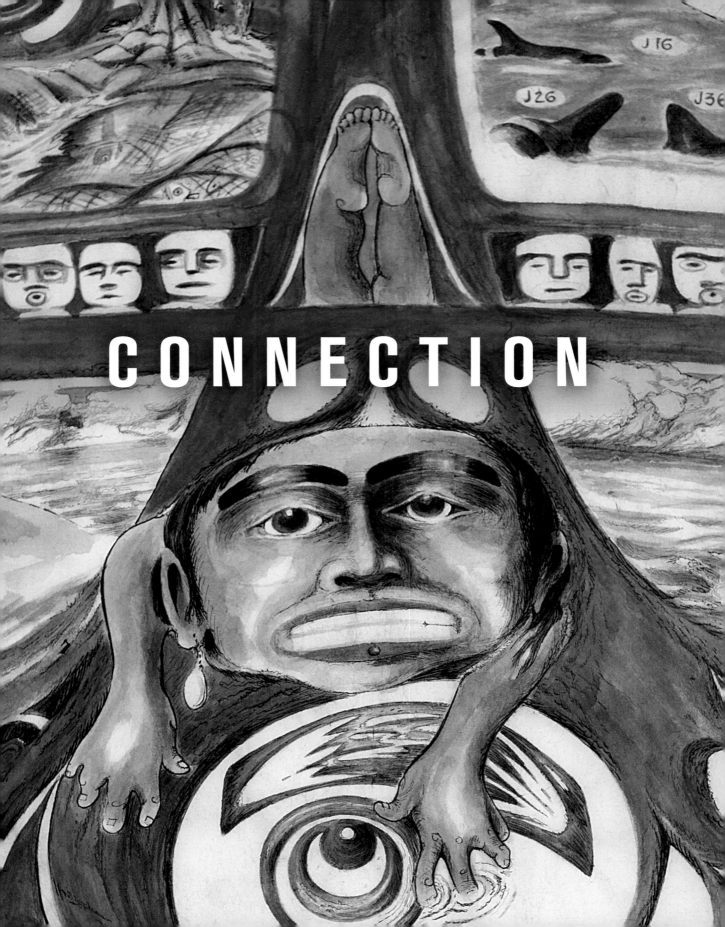

CONNECTION

J 16

J 26

J 36

SG̲aana sG̲aanagwa
Supernatural Killer Whales

AS TOLD BY

GwaaG̲anad Diane Brown, Ts'aahl Eagle woman of the Haida Nation,

to her daughter-in-law Kihlgula Gaay.ya Severn Cullis-Suzuki, Ravens of Tanu

THIS STORY WAS TOLD TO ME by Hazel Stevens a very long time ago. In 1985, during the fight for Lyell Island, as a matter of fact.

The story is about two men from the west coast of Haida Gwaii who went fishing in their food gathering canoe. Not a big canoe, two men could handle it. So they went out. Meanwhile, a bad storm hit. They didn't return. So the people started to mourn for them. They waited a year for them to come home, and when they didn't come home in a year, they held a memorial, and put them away in a good way.

However, one year after that, someone was down the beach, and they noticed something way on the horizon. Then another person noticed. Then another person. Then pretty soon they started asking, *what could it be?* Soon they saw three shapes coming toward them on the horizon, and they still couldn't figure out what it was. Finally it came right to the village. It was two killer whales guiding the canoe back, right to the same village where they left. So they got off, and everyone was rejoicing. They told the story of how they got caught in the storm, a bad storm, and they washed up in the land of the people that ate maggots. That was Japan—they ate rice.

And so they spent two years with them, they lived amongst them. But they got very, very homesick. So they started off home, on the same canoe. By nightfall, the thickest fog came. They could not see the stars. They thought they were doomed, because the fog just wasn't moving. It was like that for a day or so, and just when they were ready to give up, they heard a *xwshhhhhh*, *xwshhhhh*. Here a killer whale came swimming up to them on one side of the canoe, and stayed. They paddled along awhile, and then they heard it again, *xwshhhhhh*, in the distance. Another killer whale came to the other side of them. The killer whales guided them right to the village. Right back to where they started from.

Hazel Stevens ended the story by saying, "Those Haida men were young and strong, and they were there for two years, and you can't tell me they lived by themselves! So I believe we have relatives in Japan." That's how she ended it. That's the end of the story.

THE KILLER WHALES are very important to the Haida people.

There's the Creator, who created all things, and then there's the Supernatural Beings, and the head person of the Supernatural Beings is the killer whale. Next to God are the killer whales. That's how important they are in the scheme of things. They are so important.

My mother said, when I was a child, if you ever see whales, you clear and clean your mind, because they know what you're thinking. They are so powerful. They are feeling beings, you know. They are more feeling than us, because they are in the spirit world and they're in this world. They're of both worlds.

Even today, they are still very powerful. So in my heart I feel that if any harm came to them, that would put such a huge hole in our being. It's like taking a whole 50 chapters out of our history. I don't even know if we'd *be*. I don't know how we'd be without the killer whales. They are so big in our life. And our spirituality, and our physical being. They're in all the major stories; there are monster Killerwhales like 'wasG̱uu—the half-wolf and half–killer whale—and the five-fin Killerwhale. But even the one-fin killer whales are supernatural! So they're very important, and I was made to know that, right from a very young age. To be respectful.

So it's heartbreaking what's happening to the killer whales. And knowing that we're responsible. All of us.

It'll take all of us to change it.

That's it. ︶⟩⟩

We Need Orcas More Than They Need Us

David Suzuki

WHEN MY DAUGHTER SEVERN WAS EIGHT, I took her to the K'tzim-a-deen (Khutzeymateen) Valley in northwestern British Columbia, where I was filming a CBC *Nature of Things* program on grizzly bears. When we finished, we took the boat to Prince Rupert. An orca surfaced next to us. "Severn, come up on deck and see the whale!" I shouted as it dove. Severn clambered up, and we waited for the orca to reappear. "There it is!" I shouted when it surfaced in the distance.

I looked at Severn, expecting to see her radiant with excitement. Instead, she was weeping. "What's wrong?" I asked. "Look how far it went on one breath of air," she said, "and those whales in the aquarium are kept in a tiny tank." I was dumbstruck. A child could clearly see the problem cetaceans face in captivity. Whales and dolphins mean big crowds, and thus big money for aquariums, including, at the time, the one in our hometown of Vancouver, which we had visited often. It was the world's first aquarium to capture and display an orca—Moby Doll, in 1964.

The original intent then was to harpoon, kill and dissect the orca and create a sculpture for study and display. The orca survived, in part because two other orcas held him afloat to keep him from drowning, which showed the animals might not be the vicious killers they had been thought to be. He was held in drydock in North Vancouver, where he attracted 20,000 visitors during one day on display. Moby Doll only survived a few months in captivity, but his popularity presented an opportunity, and captive orcas and other cetaceans became a feature of the Vancouver Aquarium and other parks and aquariums.

ORCAS ARE TOUCHING PEOPLE'S HEARTS AND GRABBING HEADLINES.

Humans have been mistreating these misunderstood animals for a long time, hunting them—often because they were seen as competition for valuable fisheries resources—and keeping them captive for entertainment and profit. Now we know these mammals share many traits with humans. They are intelligent animals with complex social structures and feelings.

Research and observation have indicated they display emotions ranging from joy, fear and anger to grief and self-awareness. Biology supports the idea of emotions in orcas: their large limbic lobe and cellular architecture—spindle cells—give clues about this ability. These systems are associated with social organization and empathy and are present in many whale species, including orcas. The killer whale brain has more spindle cells than the human brain.[1] They live in "pods," which are similar to human families. The oldest female leads this highly stable pack of siblings, which are related via maternal lineage. Males seek females from other groups for breeding but return to their pods, while the calves stay with the mothers' pods. Pod members help each other in different ways, including babysitting and sharing food. It is common to see pod members other than the mother supervising and protecting a baby orca while the parent hunts for food. Even adult male orcas look after young pod members!

Orcas are also known as killer whales, even though they're not really whales but are a dolphin species. The name comes from the term Spanish seafarers gave them, *ballena asesina*, or whale assassin, based on their hunting practices. They were also known as "wolves of the sea." A large male weighs nearly as much as two F-150 pickup trucks.

Every killer whale population has its own unique culture, which includes language, social behaviours and dietary preferences. Some orca populations are more vulnerable than others. While Transient orcas thrive on seals and other marine mammals, the salmon-eating Resident orcas in the Salish Sea, near Vancouver, are dwindling. With climate change, chinook salmon in decline and human activities threatening them, their population has diminished by 20 per cent in under 20 years. Only 75 remain.

Fortunately, as we learn more about orcas, we're finally undergoing a major change in our attitude toward them. Orcas are touching people's hearts and grabbing headlines. Organizations like the David Suzuki Foundation and its partners do critical work in developing initiatives and gaining support for Salish Sea orcas. The need to save these orcas is now clear, but massive co-operation and passionate advocacy are still necessary to help people take action. We must come together and create a movement that involves government, businesses, advocacy groups and individuals.

Years of activism helped raise awareness about the plight of captive cetaceans, culminating in the release of the 2013 documentary film *Blackfish*, about captive whales, dolphins and porpoises in parks like SeaWorld in the United States. In 2018, calling the increasing outcry against captive whales a "distraction" for its conservation work and business—and following a decision by the Vancouver Park Board to prevent new whales and dolphins from being brought in—the Vancouver Aquarium decided to end its cetacean program, keeping only stranded and distressed whales and dolphins that can be rehabilitated and released back into the wild.

It's an example of how our values and beliefs can change over time. When Europeans arrived in North America, they encountered people with cultures so different they seemed incomprehensible. The new arrivals wrote the Indigenous people off as "savages," primitive because they didn't have agriculture, written language or elaborate clothing as Europeans did. Today, few people would be so cavalier toward Indigenous cultures.

The way we see our place in the world and our relationship with others evolves over time. Women in Canada were once considered unworthy of the right to vote. Indigenous people, Asian Canadians and African Canadians were denied full rights of citizenship, including the right to vote, until after the Second World War. Not long ago, homosexuality was illegal. The environmental and animal rights movements have placed our relationship with other species under scrutiny to create similar social changes.

In some respects, colonial notions and reductionist science are catching up with the unique environmental knowledge held by people Europeans once considered "savages." Although coastal Indigenous peoples hunted whales for sustenance, they viewed orcas as neighbours and, in some ways, as equals—not as resources to be governed or lesser animals meant for human entertainment. Orcas were important to their rich cultural traditions and stories.

In Western culture, governments and people were seemingly unaware of our

COMMUNITY **JESSE CAMPBELL**

ALTHOUGH HUNTING DIMINISHED, THE ORCAS' PERCEIVED ENTERTAINMENT VALUE INCREASED.

interdependence with nature, so they put natural resources foremost to human use. Historically, mainstream culture viewed orcas as adversaries. Fishers saw them as competition for fish, and the public viewed them as monsters. As a result, fishers frequently shot orcas on sight. In the early 1960s, fishing organizations led a discussion about the perceived prevalence of orcas in Discovery Passage.[2] Orcas were labelled "pests," and "remedies" were proposed. One outcome was installation of a machine gun on a lookout on Quadra Island overlooking Seymour Narrows.

It was intended to shoot as many orcas as possible. Luckily, the gun was never fired. The Department of Fisheries and Oceans was concerned that the bullets could ricochet off the water and hit someone, and that the gun could present a forest-fire hazard. Another proposed remedy that was never implemented was bombing from the air. These actions and discussions show how far the perceptions of orcas in the mid-twentieth century were from reality.

Although hunting diminished, the orcas' perceived entertainment value increased. The Vancouver Aquarium had a huge impact on me when I was a boy. It shaped some of my interests and career. I watched its whales and dolphins with wonder and awe, but eventually, seeing them perform to human dictates made me uncomfortable. Severn's response to a wild killer whale brought the issue into focus. Whales and dolphins evolved in the open ocean; they are genetically programmed to roam free over vast expanses. Yet we chose to capture, confine and train them in part for our own amusement—although many aquariums also did what they considered valuable research that they hoped would help with conservation efforts.

Proponents claimed that studying captive whales yielded invaluable information (presumably that couldn't be replicated in the wild) about communication, echolocation for food sourcing and navigation, energetics (food energy required under various conditions), gestation, diseases and health, and environmental influences such as pollution and climate change.

But the problems cetaceans face are obvious. We don't need studies on captive animals to provide that information. We

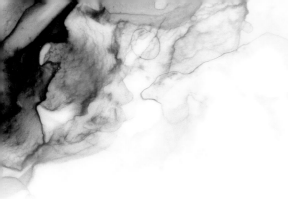

I CAN'T IMAGINE WHAT A WHALE IS CONSCIOUS OF IN A TINY TANK WITH SOUND ECHOING OFF THE WALLS. I CAN'T IMAGINE THE PHYSIOLOGICAL STATE OF AN ANIMAL SO FAR REMOVED FROM ITS NORMAL HABITAT AS TO BE CONSTANTLY STRESSED BY CONFINEMENT.

invade the animals' territory, pollute the waters not only with chemicals and waste but also with sound, and we are unwilling to protect the quality of the wildlife, water and ecosystems that the animals need to thrive. We try to force nature to fit into the priorities and demands of our species.

I can't imagine what a whale is conscious of in a tiny tank with sound echoing off the walls. I can't imagine the physiological state of an animal so far removed from its normal habitat as to be constantly stressed by confinement. My reaction as a scientist is that the data obtained from whales in captivity would be artifacts resulting from the prison in which they are kept. Scientific information? Observation in the wild didn't hold back Charles Darwin or Jane Goodall. It's a poor justification for keeping whales in captivity.

Although ending the practice of keeping cetaceans in captivity is a good start, our actions continue to create hardship for animals in the wild. In my part of the world, we now know that overfishing and climate change are depriving the Southern Resident orcas in the Salish Sea of their main dietary staple, chinook salmon. The Southern Resident population, as of early 2020, is down to 73. Despite recent protection measures implemented by the federal government, threats are increasing, especially with plans to expand the Trans Mountain pipeline to transport massive amounts of climate-altering bitumen from northern Alberta to Vancouver to be loaded onto tankers and shipped to markets in the United States and overseas.

Orcas and other cetaceans depend on echolocation, communicating and navigating using a complex "language" of sounds. Noise from marine traffic and industry makes communicating and hunting difficult. Imagine living with neighbours who turn up the music so loud that you can't hear much of anything else most of the time. Southern Resident orcas live in a similar circumstance. Sound is transmitted much more efficiently underwater, making echolocation the most useful sense for orcas. Noise from boats can make the difference between eating and starving. When salmon scarcity combines with noise, orcas can get so discouraged that they stop hunting altogether.

Climate change is also a major threat. Salmon depend on cool, clean, well-oxygenated water. Warmer waters alter the chances of chinook salmon survival and consequently diminish their ability to feed the orca. Under these circumstances, the communities that rely on the ocean for resources are walking a fine line in trying to sustain their needs while preserving the ecosystem—a hard balance to keep.

Whatever salmon the orcas do manage to catch may carry contaminants from the water. Orcas are at the apex of a complex food web, and so they acquire high doses of the toxic chemicals in the environment that accumulate in the bodies of their prey.

We've come a long way in our understanding of these magnificent animals, but will our efforts to help them be too little, too late? We now know that keeping such intelligent, large animals in captivity is wrong. But are our recent efforts to protect them and their habitat and food sources enough? We still haven't been able to stop or even slow the numerous obstacles we've put in their way, from ever-increasing shipping traffic to overfishing to pollution to climate change. Orcas are a critical part of the complex web that keeps ocean and coastal ecosystems functioning. We need them, and we must do more to ensure that they thrive and survive long into the future. ✑

Notes

1   Crawford, Lars. "Killer Whales Are Non-Human Persons." *Grey Matters Journal*, 13 Dec. 2013, greymattersjournal.com/killer-whales-are-non-human-persons

2   "A Brief History of the Southern Residents." Georgia Strait Alliance, georgiastrait.org/work/species-at-risk/orca-protection/southern-resident-orcas/brief-history-southern-residents

THE WHALE FAMILY TREE RAY TROLL

A Bond Through Salmon, Language and Grandmothers

Misty MacDuffee

CULTURE IS DEFINED as information or behaviour that is shared within a community and transmitted within or between generations through social learning. Culture has always been considered the unique hallmark of human societies. Until recently, the concept had never been ascribed to animals. However, as scientists are recognizing that decades of conservation strategies have failed to identify and account for key aspects of animal societies, this is rapidly changing. Lessons from fish to birds to mammals have shown the importance of social learning.

Some people's first contact with animal culture might have been the stories of human guidance provided via ultralight aircraft to assist cranes and geese raised in captivity that learn their migration routes socially. It is seen in bighorn sheep and moose that have been reintroduced to areas and then take generations to determine the seasonal availability of high-quality food. Many now know that a healthy elephant population requires elders to influence the behaviour and the development of younger animals. Even reef fish learn to identify predators without direct experience through socially transmitted information. These transfers of behaviour and knowledge lead to improved survival. The resilience of cultural diversity, along with genetics, appears key to the persistence and resilience of a wide range of animal populations.

The Southern Resident killer whales that ply the waters of coastal British Columbia and the Pacific Northwest are often distinguished from other ecotypes of killer whales based on their unique diet, dialect and culture. Vocal dialects, the differences in communication calls between neighbouring groups of whales, were one of the first recognized forms

VOCAL DIALECTS, THE DIFFERENCES IN COMMUNICATION CALLS BETWEEN NEIGHBOURING GROUPS OF WHALES, WERE ONE OF THE FIRST RECOGNIZED FORMS OF CULTURE IN KILLER WHALES.

of culture in killer whales. Calves learn their dialect from their mothers and other family members. They retain it for life, and they pass it on to the next generation. Groups of whales with similar dialects are considered more closely related. Among the Southern Residents, the different pods (J, K and L) can be vocally distinguished based on the subtle differences in their calls. Researchers think these socially learned dialects might be important for female killer whales to distinguish males from outside their pods and thus avoid inbreeding. As a larger clan (J clan), the Southern Residents have calls that can be distinguished from those of the Northern and Alaskan Resident clans.

Culture in these whales is also observed through the presence of menopause, another biological process that we typically think of as a human trait. When Granny, the matriarch of J pod, a Southern Resident killer whale family group, died in 2016, she was believed to be more than 90 years old, but she hadn't had a calf in more than 50 years. The researchers who viewed

hundreds of hours of video footage found that in years when salmon abundance was low, the movements of whales were led by the post-reproductive females, for these were the whales with the greatest knowledge of where to look for salmon. The grandmothers are the repositories of ecological knowledge.

Viewing a map of the distribution of Resident killer whale clans on the Pacific coast of North America shows us an overlap with the distribution of another iconic symbol of the West Coast, Pacific salmon. From northern California to Alaska, the range of these salmon-eating killer whales aligns with the spawning rivers of their primary prey.

The J clan of Resident killer whales occupy the most southern of the eastern Pacific distribution, earning them their "Southern Resident" moniker. Their hunting grounds cover the migration routes of chinook salmon, ranging from as far south as Monterey Bay to Vancouver Island and the Salish Sea in the north. But to find chinook salmon, whales need to know more than *where* to look for them—they also need to know *when* to look. More than any other salmon species, chinook throughout this range can be found returning to their natal rivers almost any month of the year. One river system, the Sacramento–San Joaquin River in California's central valley, had runs of adult chinook every month of the year. The spring portion of these runs was often the largest and usually began in March. In the Central Valley, the first chinook to arrive in the spring run overlapped with the last arrivals of the winter run. Killer whales would have known that heading to California in the late winter was a good bet.

The biggest chinook river systems in North America were north of California's Central Valley. The largest, the Columbia basin, drains much of western North America. The next largest is Canada's Fraser River watershed, draining one-quarter of British Columbia. Big rivers, with riverbeds of course gravel and cobble, host big chinook salmon. The gravel stream beds are used by spawning salmon as nurseries, where fertilized eggs buried

by the female will lie protected in a redd (nest) just below the typical scour force of the river. Few eggs are crushed or washed away under typical conditions, and those hidden in the gravel receive the oxygen necessary to grow. The structure of the gravel beds is so ideal for the developing embryos, it's as if the salmon designed it themselves. And indeed they did. The sheer size and number of the chinook salmon that moved huge volumes of rock, determining the river width, the gravel bars, and the overall structure of the river, engineered these spawning grounds. They designed the nursery with the right water depth, water velocities and gravel size. And for thousands and thousands of years, this strategy usually prevailed.

There are several possible reasons that Southern Resident killer whales evolved to select chinook over the other salmon species as their preferred choice of prey. They will eat other salmon, especially species like chum, steelhead and coho, but chinook are preferred. Chinook are the largest of all salmon and have the highest fat content. They are also available within Resident

THERE ARE SEVERAL POSSIBLE REASONS THAT SOUTHERN RESIDENT KILLER WHALES EVOLVED TO SELECT CHINOOK OVER THE OTHER SALMON SPECIES AS THEIR PREFERRED CHOICE OF PREY.

killer whale foraging grounds year-round. Their large size and high fat content make pursuing chinook a much more efficient expenditure of energy than pursuing smaller pink or sockeye salmon, even though smaller salmon are more abundant.

Large chinook can also be shared with family members, which is the typical way for the Southern Residents to consume them. Sharing is most common between a mother and her calf, but it is observed among all family members. The sharing of food reinforces the strong bonds that exist between family members, and feeding co-operation improves the chances of survival at an individual level and as a genetically unique matriline of Resident killer whales. Killer whale scientists think sharing may also limit greed, aggression and competition among family members.

So for thousands of years a Southern Resident killer whale lineage would have lived as a tightly knit unit with all the members of the mother's family. An individual male whale could have a mother, grandmother, aunts and uncles, siblings, nieces and nephews. Living with his family, especially the presence of his mother, improved the likelihood that this male whale would survive. The family would travel and feed together, they would breed and socialize with other matrilines of whale families within the larger clan, they would teach young whales the communication calls unique to their family group, they would learn the timing and locations of salmon runs so that food could always be found, and they would pass the knowledge and the behaviours on to their offspring, and so forth through the generations.

But in the last 100 years, much of this has changed.

The context for the plight of Southern Residents today was underway by the mid-twentieth century. How many whales there were before this is unknown, but preliminary genetic examinations suggest a population of fewer than 200. Little was known about killer whales by the European colonists of the day. There was

REMARKABLY, THERE WAS A PERIOD AT THE END OF THE TWENTIETH CENTURY WHEN WHALE NUMBERS WERE GROWING. WHY THEY FALTERED AFTER THIS IS NOT CLEAR, BUT A GROWING BODY OF RESEARCH IS PAINTING A PICTURE OF MULTIPLE THREATS THAT INTENSIFY WHEN FOOD IS LIMITED.

A chinook salmon in the lower Fraser River, 2018. April Bencze/ Raincoast photo.

no distinction of ecotypes with different diets, let alone clans, pods, matrilines or individuals. There was no estimate of numbers. Killer whales did not enjoy the broad appeal they do today.

Removal of killer whales for the aquarium trade began in 1961. In total, 68 whales were taken from southern BC and Washington waters, 47 of which were later determined to be Southern Residents. It wasn't until after the practice ended in 1977 that awareness of their distinct behaviour, their small numbers, and their uniqueness as the Pacific coast's most southerly population of salmon-eating killer whales emerged. But by this time, the damage was done.

Between the aquarium trade and an unknown number lost to gunshot wounds acquired in fishery conflicts, the population dropped below 70 whales. This had long-lasting biological effects in terms of the small size of the remaining population and the lost generation: most of the removals were juveniles. The removals likely had

cultural effects as well, in terms of the loss of strong bonds and the social cohesion that existed between family members. Anyone who has watched footage of the capture process might describe these as abductions.

Remarkably, there was a period at the end of the twentieth century when whale numbers were growing. Why they faltered after this is not clear, but a growing body of research is painting a picture of multiple threats that intensify when food is limited. Dr. John Ford at Canada's Pacific Biological Station led the seminal work that established the relationship between Resident killer whales and chinook salmon. Ford and his team found that in years when the overall abundance of chinook was higher, birth rates were higher and mortality was lower. The opposite holds as well: when chinook abundance declined, so did birth rates, and mortality increased.

The declining abundance of chinook may not be the only factor affecting whales. Chinook are also getting smaller, so more salmon are needed to meet a killer whale's caloric demands, and more energy is spent catching smaller fish. The year-round presence of migrating chinook is also becoming an artifact of the past. Serious declines in the spring and early summer abundance of chinook in the Salish Sea correlate with a decreased presence of Southern Residents in places and times where their occurrence was once very predictable.

Chinook numbers have declined, fish are smaller and spawning runs are less reliable at the same time as the Salish Sea has become a noisy and sometimes congested place. The increase in noise is especially troubling if you are an animal that relies on sound to hunt, navigate, find mates and communicate. For a Resident killer whale, survival in a world where light is limited depends on the ability to hear and be heard far more than the ability to see. The presence of vessels—from pleasure craft to fishing and whale-watching boats to ferries and international freighters—can affect killer whale communication, behaviour and survival.

Scientific approaches to understanding the effects of underwater noise on a spectrum of marine organisms have advanced significantly in the last decade. It now appears that species less complex than whales are adversely affected by noise. Animals from cephalopods, such as octopus and squid, through to zooplankton and fish have sensitive apparatuses for sensing their environment and enabling them to find food, communicate, swim, detect predators and survive. Noise can interfere with these critical functions. It can mask important communication, affect feeding, induce stress, inhibit development, cause injury, lower reproductive success and even cause death. Air-gun pulses used in seismic arrays, for example, have been shown to kill zooplankton within a one-kilometre radius of a single blast.

Global and local studies on the world's oceans indicate that underwater noise has increased by three decibels every 10 years since the 1950s. Decibels are measured on a logarithmic scale, so this translates to a doubling in ambient noise every decade for the last 70 years. Most of this noise is from increases in commercial shipping. The low-frequency sounds from ocean-going freighters and tankers can travel underwater for hundreds of kilometres, making this the principal source of ambient ocean noise. Oceanographer Dr. Scott Veirs has documented the noise from ships travelling through the Salish Sea to reach ports in the greater Vancouver and Seattle areas. These ships emit noise in a range of frequencies, including ones that overlap with frequencies used by killer whales. Even though the distance that high frequency sounds propagate from ships in the open ocean is

RESULTS FROM FOUR YEARS OF DATA SHOWED THE SIX-DECIBEL REDUCTION IN BACKGROUND NOISE POST-9/11 CORRESPONDED TO A DECREASE IN STRESS HORMONES WITHIN THE WHALES, LINKING NOISE TO CHRONIC STRESS.

generally less than 10 kilometres, once in the confined waters of the Salish Sea, mid- and high-frequency noise can quickly permeate the narrow straits and channels. And once in the Salish Sea, commercial ships are among dozens of vessel types and sources that make underwater noise ubiquitous.

In killer whales, underwater noise and vessel traffic can have several pathways of effects. As the din of underwater noise grows, the area over which killer whales can hear and be heard decreases. This loss of *communication space* requires a whale to be closer to detect prey. The shorter the detection range, the less probable it is that the whale will find a salmon. Evidence also shows that killer whales respond to the noise by increasing the amplitude of their calls, requiring more energy to be heard.

Noise may impart stress as well. The tragic events of 9/11 in 2001 led to a remarkable opportunity for scientists studying North Atlantic Right whales in the Bay of Fundy. A scat collection study was underway at the time, examining stress-related hormones in the whales. In the days following 9/11, underwater noise was significantly reduced from the grounding of ship and air traffic. Results from four years of data showed the six-decibel reduction in background noise post-9/11 corresponded to a decrease in stress hormones within the whales, linking noise to chronic stress.

Noise from vessels can also mask echolocation clicks killer whales use to detect and catch their prey. Killer whales distinguish chinook salmon from other salmon based on the sonar echoes bouncing off the salmon's swim bladder, an organ that can reflect 90 per cent of the sound energy directed at it. A chinook's swim bladder is smaller than that of a coho or sockeye and differs enough for orcas to detect and discriminate single chinook at distances of more than 100 metres. A hungry killer whale determines the species and size of the salmon, its direction, and how fast it's moving by sending rapid sequences of clicks and listening for their echo. Boat noise in the frequencies used by the whale can mask these critical echoes.

Lastly, the physical presence of a vessel in close proximity to a hunting killer

Aerial photograph of a group of Southern Resident killer whales chasing a salmon, 2017. Image collected non-invasively during scientific research using a hexacopter drone at an altitude of over 100 feet above the whales, with research authorized by NMFS permit 19091. Photo by John Durban (NOAA), Holly Fearnbach (SR3) and Lance Barrett-Lennard (Coastal Ocean Research Institute).

whale can interfere with the chase. Dr. Rob Williams has studied the way boats can disrupt Resident killer whale behaviour and activities (like feeding, socializing, resting or travelling). His work indicates that the combination of physical and acoustic disturbance from the vessel can reduce feeding success by up to 25 per cent. Estimates of vessel exposure for Southern Resident killer whales inside the Salish Sea suggest Southern Residents are in the presence of vessels 85 per cent of the time and foraging in the presence of vessels 78 per cent of the time. This translates to a 16 per cent reduction in their food consumption when they are using their summer feeding grounds.

When chinook are abundant, the consequence of lost meals to noise and disturbance can likely be endured, at least to some degree. The effort expended to catch a meal is critical when chinook abundance is low. From ending a five-minute food chase to avoid a boat that was originally 200 metres away to the salmon that escaped because propeller cavitation masked echolocation clicks, it only takes a few minutes of interference at crucial times to lose a meal. Noise and disturbance reduces a killer whale's hunting success, and for the Southern Residents, that means eating fewer salmon. Returning to Dr. Ford's early conclusions: fewer chinook salmon mean fewer calves born and increases in adult mortality.

Food-stressed whales also have to contend with another ugly side of the human footprint in the Salish Sea: pollution.

Chinook salmon should be providing the energy and nutrition to fuel survival and population growth, but they also deliver toxins accumulated from feeding in waters that drain the lands where eight million people live, work and recreate—the watersheds of the Salish Sea. Studies done on Puget Sound Chinook salmon have documented a suite of chemical contaminants that stretch from metals and toxins carried from cars and roads in stormwater, to pharmaceutical and recreational drugs delivered in wastewater. They also have industrial legacy pollutants (such as flame retardants, PCBs and DDT) that persist and bioaccumulate through food webs even though their use has been regulated. These fat-loving toxins accumulate in salmon, and then in whales through their salmon diet, building up in lipid-rich tissues like blubber and in milk.

Food-stressed whales burn their fat reserves. When they do, they likely mobilize the persistent pollutants stored in their fat. In a mother, contaminants stored in milk are transferred to a nursing calf. These pollutants can act as hormone mimics and unleash developmental effects in a foetus or a calf. Toxins in food-stressed whales are the likely reason for the excessively high rates of failed pregnancies in

Southern Residents. Between 2008 and 2014, only 11 out of 33 pregnancies were successful, a failure rate of 69 per cent. In 2017 and 2018 there were no successful calves at all.

But lack of births is only part of the problem. A 2017 genetic study found that only two males fathered half the Southern Resident calves born since 1990 and that breeding within matrilines is occurring. This raises concerns for inbreeding, genetic diversity and fitness of offspring. There is also concern for skewed sex ratios that favour males.

But the more immediate problem is keeping existing whales alive. Since being listed as endangered under Canada's Species at Risk Act in 2003, more than 50 whales have died, most of whom should have survived for much longer. Drone images of body condition collected by the Vancouver Aquarium and its US partners have revealed whales visibly malnourished, including the extreme loss of fat around the cranium that characterizes a condition called "peanut-head." Rarely do whales recover once these signs appear.

Combined, the lack of births and high mortality mean the population is not just failing to grow; it is declining at a rate that could spell extinction within 100 years. Some unique matrilines already show dead ends, with no reproductive females in the wings. Remember, however, it's not just a numbers game: cultural knowledge, especially that held by mature females, is essential to everyone's survival.

The events that unfolded in the summer of 2018 galvanized many people to think about the Salish Sea, our human footprint and the iconic sentinels of these waters in a manner they had not before. The year started with 77 killer whales. The primary threats to recovery were widely known and conveyed in one sentence: reduced prey availability, physical and acoustic disturbance from vessels, and contaminant exposure. Addressing these threats means confronting our human activities: fishing, whale watching, shipping, watershed planning, human consumption, population growth and climate change. Herein lies the inertia, in the aspirations of a large, affluent human population and

COMBINED, THE LACK OF BIRTHS AND HIGH MORTALITY MEAN THE POPULATION IS NOT JUST FAILING TO GROW; IT IS DECLINING AT A RATE THAT COULD SPELL EXTINCTION WITHIN 100 YEARS.

CANADA'S STEPS TOWARD THREAT REDUCTION STARTED AFTER MOUNTING PUBLIC PRESSURE OVER DELAYED RECOVERY ACTION, LAWSUITS, THE GROWING PROFILE OF WHALE DEATHS AND DECLINING NUMBERS FORCED ACTION.

the consequential social and economic implications of any measures.

In the state of Washington, Governor Jay Inslee struck a special task force instructed to make recommendations for recovery measures. From Washington State's perspective, struggling killer whales reflect the health of the Salish Sea. From forage fish like the herring that feed chinook salmon to pollutants draining into Puget Sound, the problems stem from the loss of ecosystem function, a concept that links ecosystem components (species) and processes to the quality and quantity of habitat. Ecosystem function is fundamental to the survival of endangered species, and its benefits accrue to far more than one species.

The Washington State Legislature, guided by Governor Inslee's task force, subsequently passed stronger laws to protect fish habitat and passed new toxin laws that allow for regulation of whole classes of household toxic chemicals. Environmental groups have called this the nation's strongest legislation for consumer products.

Canada's steps toward threat reduction started after mounting public pressure over delayed recovery action, lawsuits, the growing profile of whale deaths and declining numbers forced action. The first federal measures were seasonal sport fishing closures in some places where Southern Residents feed. The goal was to reduce competition, noise and disturbance from fishing vessels in pursuit of the same chinook salmon. This was followed with more vessel measures. The distance boats had to maintain from a pod was increased to 400 metres. Sanctuaries were proposed (prohibiting vessels), and shipping companies were encouraged to slow down to limit their noise. Canada's approach is species specific, linking threats to explicit times and areas. Although ostensibly comprehensive, these efforts fall short. Broadly, the times, areas and reductions are limited relative to what is likely necessary to effectively reduce stressors on whales. Importantly, most measures are not regulatory. That said, it marks a start.

Washington and Canada have taken different approaches to threat reduction. Both are necessary. What neither jurisdiction has accomplished is a way to increase chinook abundance, largely because viewpoints on why Southern Residents aren't getting enough to eat are divided. Hatcheries are often touted as a solution, but putting more money and effort into hatchery production at a time when evidence indicates hatcheries are part of the reason wild chinook have failed to recover only deepens the problem. Southern Residents evolved to target large and old chinook salmon that spread their spawning migration from spring to fall. Hatcheries have failed to restore the old ages, big sizes, migration times and diversity of wild chinook salmon. While this is worsened by fishing and climate change, new science suggests that the billions of hatchery salmon released annually into the North Pacific are overgrazing the commons. There simply isn't enough food to go around, and chinook may be bigger losers in this game than, say, pink salmon. Whatever the mechanism, the evidence shows that the more hatchery fish there are, the less likely it is wild chinook will recover.

But what chinook hatcheries do accomplish is keeping fisheries open, and therein lies a principal controversy in Southern Resident killer whale recovery. From Alaska to the Pacific Northwest, more than a million chinook destined for Southern Resident feeding grounds are caught legally in marine fisheries. In addition, unknown numbers die from *encounters* with legal fisheries and as by-catch in non-salmon fisheries.

Fish-eating seals and sea lions also are blamed for eating chinook. While pinniped numbers have grown since their protection in the 1970s, studies show that salmon generally, and chinook specifically, are a small proportion of their diet. Further, more seals have attracted their primary predator: the mammal-eating Bigg's killer whales, an effective presence for moderating seal numbers.

In June of 2018, as Canada was announcing its first threat reduction measures, a 23-year-old male whale from L pod named Cruiser (L92) was declared dead. He had not been seen since the previous fall, and as is typical, his body was never recovered, and the cause of his death is undetermined. Population 76. In August, a juvenile whale named Scarlet (J50) was gravely ill. Named in honour of the toothmark scars on her dorsal fin, potentially from whales serving as midwives in the birthing process, Scarlet was one of the last whales born in 2015 before a three-year abeyance. As Scarlet's health declined, unprecedented efforts to save this young female were initiated, including darting her with antibiotics and releasing live chinook from a boat in front of her. Despite this, Scarlet disappeared, and her body was not recovered. Population 75.

Many have wondered if these endangered whales have passed a critical

MANY HAVE WONDERED IF THESE ENDANGERED WHALES HAVE PASSED A CRITICAL THRESHOLD IN THEIR VIABILITY TO RECOVER.

threshold in their ability to recover. In 2017, a team of scientists working with the Raincoast Conservation Foundation published a study addressing this specific question: can they recover? The team concluded that with an increase in salmon, they could, but the level of chinook required to do so was at the highest observed in the previous 30 years. Alternatively, if chinook abundance was not quite as high, but noise levels were cut in half, these endangered whales could reverse their decline and rebuild their numbers.

In July of 2018, a young mother from J pod named Tahlequah (J35) was ready to give birth. Her immediate family included her eight-year-old son, her mother, two siblings and a niece. On July 18, Tahlequah gave birth to a female calf, but by the time observers from the Center for Whale Research arrived on site, the calf was dead. Tahlequah was repeatedly bringing the small neonate to the surface and taking long dives to retrieve it when it fell from where it was balanced on the rostrum section of her head. She continued to carry her calf for 17 days.

Loss is something Southern Resident killer whales know well. Tahlequah, for example, had lost her sister two years earlier, in 2016, and her nephew shortly after that. Before this, she would have witnessed her sister lose a calf in early 2013. This was also not Tahlequah's first lost calf. There was one, and likely two, before this loss.

In his book *Beyond Words*, Dr. Carl Safina explores the tight bonds that lead to grief and emotion in animals, a topic that academics like Drs. Marc Bekoff and Barbara King have observed and documented for some time. King defines grief as a situation where surviving individuals who knew the deceased alter their behavioural routine. Regardless of the science, the inability of this mother to let go of her calf triggered a groundswell of emotion around the world, including in parents who recognize grief over a child. A remarkable documentation of these sentiments lives in a story and podcast by *Seattle Times* journalist Lynda Mapes.

Ensuring the survival of these whales in the Salish Sea isn't about managing the ocean, it's about managing humans. For a Resident killer whale, survival depends

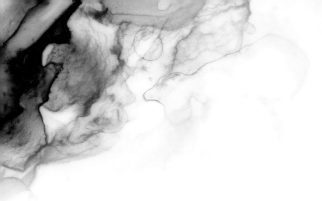

ENSURING THE SURVIVAL OF THESE WHALES IN THE SALISH SEA ISN'T ABOUT MANAGING THE OCEAN, IT'S ABOUT MANAGING HUMANS.

on the ability to hear and be heard far more than the ability to see. They now need us not just to see their plight and empathize, but to listen, and to act. Science does offer hope, indicating that we can put these whales on a trajectory toward recovery. Given this truth, we would all do well to reflect on our own ability to take responsibility for what is evident before us, as we also share a bond to this place, these salmon and these killer whales.

As night fell on that summer day in 2018 when Tahlequah gave birth to her fated calf, she and members of her matriline approached Eagle Cove on the southwest side of San Juan Island. An island resident reported what they had witnessed that evening to the Center for Whale Research. It read as follows:

"At sunset, a group of 5–6 females gathered at the mouth of the cove in a close, tight-knit circle, staying at the surface in a harmonious circular motion for nearly two hours. As the light dimmed, I was able to watch them continue what seemed to be a ritual or ceremony. They stayed directly centered in the moonbeam, even as it moved. The lighting was too dim to see if the baby was still being kept afloat. It was both sad and special to witness this behaviour. My heart goes out to J35 and her beautiful baby; bless its soul." ➳

The Peace Treaty

Rande Cook, K'alapa

This is the original story as told by the late Chief 'Maxwayalis of the Ma'a̱mtagila people. This is the tribe I am from, my chief's name is 'M̱akwa̱la (moon), I come from the house Hamatam, House of the Seagull. We are one clan out of the three that make up the Ma'a̱mtagila of today, and we still honour this treaty made in ancient times.

AFTER THE FIRST ANCESTORS descended from the heavens and built their first houses, it was the forests and the oceans they gave way for life to evolve. As life began and the many species of animals began to flourish, they taught us about unity and ways of living within harmony; there was a balance between us as humans and other life forms; there was respect.

The ma̱x̱inux̱w (orcas) controlled the seas and guided humankind in safety; they shared and taught humans about their ways. One of these ways was a system of governance, the way pods swim together and care for each other. This system was carried forth and soon became clans of each tribe, with a system in place from head chiefs to sub chiefs to commoners.

We have so much to be grateful for with the orca. We have so much that needs to be given back for their safety. Carvings of orcas often have elements of human form within them; this is the peace that we have shared since our early beginnings. The balance needed today is spiritual guidance, a more profound understanding of their significance.

For this I thank our ancestors of the past who have paved the way for us to help in protecting this beautiful species, and hopefully the orcas will continue to help educate us for many more years to come.

Gilakas'la,

Chief 'M̱akwa̱la, Ma'a̱mtagila tribe, Hamatam house, Kwakwa̱ka̱'wakw Nation

PEACE TREATY WITH THE KILLER WHALES

AS TOLD BY **Chief 'Maxwayalis Charlie Matilpi**
TO **Chief 'Makwala Rande Cook**

A LONG TIME AGO, in the beginning of our Kwakwaka'wakw history, there was a time when man and the killer whales did not live in harmony. At this time both man and whales hunted each other. It was a time of fear and great pain between both groups. There was a young boy from the Ma'amtagila tribe who treated the whales kindly, and eventually he befriended the whales.

In these ancient times, the whales and the boy could communicate, and they were able to discuss what their concerns were. The whales and the boy felt that when they hunted each other, their losses were too great, and they needed a way to end this heartache.

So the whales and the boy made a promise that they would no longer hurt each other, and have a common respect. They also thought it was important to help each other in times to come. So they discussed this arrangement, and the boy brought these plans back to his people.

The Ma'amtagila people held a meeting and decided this was in their best interest, for the whales were a powerful force and man suffered great losses in this fight also. Then, the boy was sent to bring this agreement of peace back to the whales. So a treaty was made between the killer whales and our people, and it is said that this was the first of its kind.

Still today the Kwakwaka'wakw people honour this treaty, and we have lived in harmony with the whales ever since. There are many stories telling of the killer whales saving our people when drowning, and showing the people where to find food in times of famine. ꙮ

(*Facing page*) **PEACE TREATY** **RANDE COOK**

SMALL CRAFT WARNING **CHRISTIAN GEISSLER**

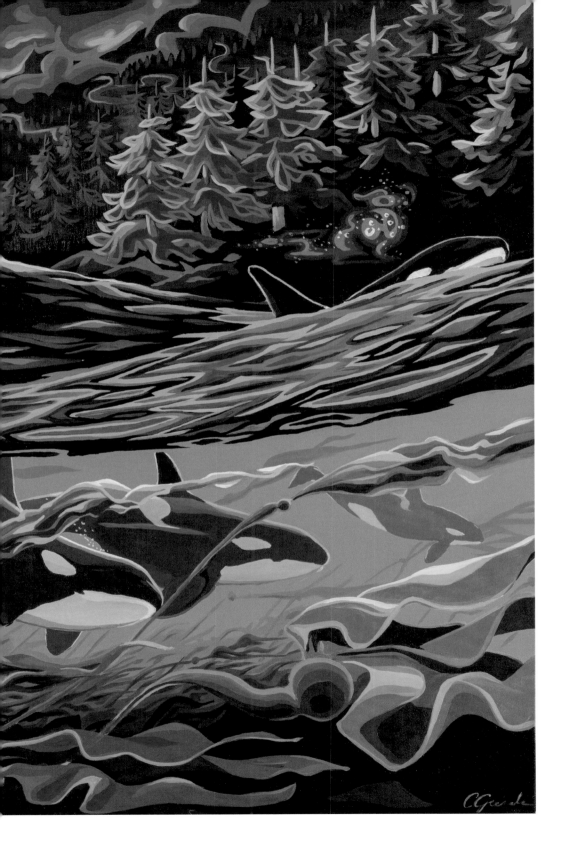

The Ocean People
Orcas as Symbols

Martha Black

WORKING ON THE EXHIBITION *ORCAS: OUR SHARED FUTURE*, I learned many things from my colleagues. Their orca knowledge comes from extensive scientific and historical research, as well as from personal experience with actual orcas in the wild and in captivity. In contrast, I have no knowledge about orcas from any of these perspectives. I have never seen an orca in an aquarium and have never been whale watching, though I did see the orca named Luna close up during trips on MV *Uchuck* down Muchalat Inlet from the Gold River dock to Yuquot (see Briony Penn's essay in this book, pages 166–171). The dramatic narrative of Luna, or Tsu'xiit, elegiac in its tragic ending, contains within it an anthropomorphic view of the whale, whose apparent need for human contact was commonly interpreted as loneliness such as we feel.

Although I know little about living orcas, I'm aware of orcas as symbols. Symbolic orcas are everywhere these days. They are symbols of stop-the-pipeline, climate change, anti-fish-farming, oceans, nature itself, ourselves. They are a recurring topic in the news cycle, usually as symbols of what's wrong with the natural world. They are a testament to the apparent helplessness of humans and of impending doom. They are also symbols of place, of Indigenous territories and of our place here on the coast of British Columbia. They are associated with specific coastal landforms in Haida Gwaii, for example. They are recognizable symbols of local communities (Alert Bay, Home of the Killer Whale), of sports teams (Vancouver Canucks) and businesses (Orca Book Publishers), and also of Indigenous ceremonial societies, clans and histories. We wear orca images on our clothing and our skin. They are symbolically our selves. To paraphrase a definition of anthropomorphism,

THESE CULTURAL BELONGINGS CAN BE THOUGHT OF IN TERMS OF SYNECDOCHE, THAT IS, AS PARTS THAT STAND IN FOR WHOLES—FOR COMPLETE SETS OF REGALIA, COMPLEX ORAL HISTORIES, LAWS AND OBLIGATIONS, WEALTH, LANDS, NAMES, SONGS, ANCESTORS, FAMILY RELATIONSHIPS AND PHILOSOPHIES.

the world of the orcas has become an imitative projection of our own world.

Anthropomorphism is defined as ascribing human form or attributes to a being or thing not human, especially to a deity, or making a non-human being or thing resemble a human form, as in an anthropomorphic carving. Indigenous Northwest Coast representations are not anthropomorphic in this sense, though. The world of orcas may be an imitative projection of the human world, but it works the other way, too. For Indigenous peoples of the Northwest Coast, the human world is a reflection of the world under the sea, the realm of the Killer Whales, which are the most powerful of the Ocean People. They are messengers of the Chief of the Undersea World, a supernatural being whose name is Ḵonanḵada in Haida, ḵumugwe' in Kwakʼwala and Qvúmúqva in Haíłzaqv (Heiltsuk), who brings wealth to anyone who sees it rising from the sea in the form of a great house.

My perspective on orcas, I realize, comes almost entirely from works of art. Since my research focuses on museum collections, I typically encounter those works not in their original cultural contexts but in museum or gallery settings, and many of the artworks through which I encounter orcas are Indigenous and from the Northwest Coast. These cultural belongings can be thought of in terms of synecdoche, that is, as parts that stand in for wholes—for complete sets of regalia, complex oral histories, laws and obligations, wealth, lands, names, songs, ancestors, family relationships and philosophies. In museum collections they become parts of non-Indigenous histories as well, symbolic of differences in understanding and categorizing the world.

One Killer Whale headdress in the collection of the Royal BC Museum (fig. 1) is a symbol of Kwakwa̱ka̱'wakw identity and chiefly status, and an embodiment of wealth, both tangible and intangible. Its double fin suggests supernatural powers

Figure 1. Kwakwa̱ka̱'wakw Killer Whale headdress. RBCM 12344.

The Royal BC Museum acquired the headdress along with a button blanket (RBCM 12357) in 1965. At that time both were in the possession of Mildred Valley Thornton, an artist and journalist based in Vancouver who had a particular interest in First Nations cultures and painted portraits of many Indigenous people throughout British Columbia and Alberta. The headdress and blanket were accessioned into the museum's collection with no accompanying information about their original owner or where and from whom Thornton might have acquired them, but we know from photographs taken by Charles F. Newcombe in 1899 that both once belonged to the family of Charles Nowell, a Kwakwa̱ka̱'wakw chief originally from Tsax̱is (Fort Rupert) (fig. 2). The headdress and blanket had come to Nowell through his marriage to Ruth, the daughter of Chief Lagius, in 1899. A number of photographs in the museum collection show Chief Lagius, Ruth Lagius Nowell and Charles Nowell wearing the headress and blanket, apart and together, over a period of at least 25 years (figs. 3 through 6). These images hint at how, in its original cultural context, the Killer Whale headdress signified identity, lineage, connections and collective action.

Mildred Valley Thornton likely acquired the headdress and blanket in 1946 when she painted a portrait of Charles Nowell wearing them, probably at the

of the ocean beings. It proclaims ancestral connections with those powerful beings, the transfer of property through marriage between lineages, and enduring connections with family and place. Although now physically housed in the museum, its connection to the descendants of the distinguished Kwakwa̱ka̱'wakw chiefs who wore it continues. A powerful work of art by a carver, perhaps from Alert Bay, it may link to an entire oeuvre by that artist, whose name does not appear in museum records. Eventually it became associated with a non-Indigenous artist—whose name, in contrast to that of the carver who has been made anonymous, does appear in the records—for whom it symbolized a personal avocation.

Charley at Seventy

Figure 2 (left). Portrait of Charles Nowell in *Smoke From Their Fires: The Life of a Kwakiutl Chief*, 1941.

Figure 3 (below). Chief Lagius carried ashore in a canoe at the marriage of his daughter to Charles Nowell, 1899. RBCM PN 2614.

likely have had regalia with him in Vancouver. Perhaps he also posed for his portrait in the tent at Kitsilano.

Three years after she painted Charles Nowell wearing his regalia, Mildred Valley Thornton herself posed, very dramatically, wearing the same headdress and button blanket for a photograph that was published in the *Vancouver Sun* (fig.7). (She was the *Sun*'s art critic at the time.) A disconcerting image of cultural appropriation, the photograph bears witness to the migration of the

Pacific National Exhibition in Vancouver.[1] A portrait of Chief Dan Cranmer from Alert Bay wearing his frontlet and button blanket was painted there in 1946.[2] Cranmer was the announcer for public performances of what was billed as the Cedar Bark Dance Ceremony at the PNE that year and sat for his portrait in a tent at the Kitsilano fairgrounds. If Nowell was among the people from Alert Bay taking part in the dance performances, he would

Figure 4 (facing page). Ruth Lagius Nowell, Charles Nowell and Mrs. Lagius, 1899. RBCM PN 994.

Figure 5 (top). Mrs. Nowell's blanket is at left, and the tunic and Killer Whale headdress third from right in this photograph taken during the McKenna-McBride Royal Commission visit to Alert Bay, 1914. RBCM PN 2786.

Figure 6 (bottom). Charles Nowell, third from left, in a group photograph taken at Alert Bay about 1924. RBCM PN 2318.

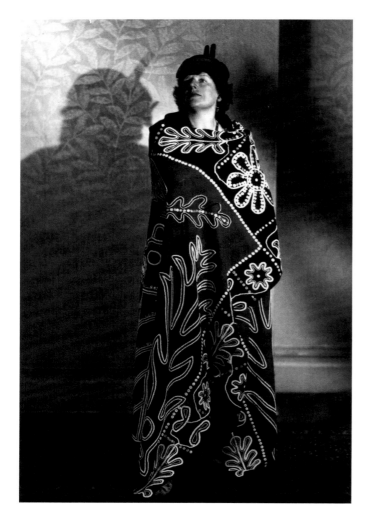

Figure 7. Mildred Valley Thornton wears the Nowell blanket and Killer Whale headdress in a photograph published in the *Vancouver Sun*, 1949. Material republished with the express permission of Vancouver Sun, a division of Postmedia Network Inc.

colourful material for my brush," and this photograph would seem to illustrate that perspective. Yet at the same time she expressed her "enduring respect" for Indigenous peoples and their histories, arts, ways of life and spirituality,[4] suggesting she felt kinship with these values. The button blanket and the red and black cloth hat to which the wooden Killer Whale fin is attached remind us of the historical Indigenous tradition of incorporating selected materials of non-Indigenous origin into Indigenous belongings and transforming them into symbols of Indigenous identity. In contrast, Thornton incorporates the Killer Whale headdress and blanket into her artwork and then makes them symbolic of her own identity and avocation. By posing in Charles Nowell's regalia, with his Killer Whale crest, she dramatizes some sort of idealized personal transformation.

Indigenous cultures well understand the transformative powers of killer whales, both symbolic and actual. The Nuu-chah-nulth (nuučaan̓uɫ) people of the west coast of Vancouver Island say that when wolves go into the sea, they transform into killer whales to hunt in the sea, and when killer whales come out of the sea, they become wolves to hunt on the land (fig. 8).[5] This transformation reflects similarities between the group hunting behaviours of wolves and orcas, but it also highlights the nuučaan̓uɫ concept of hishuk ish ts'awalk,

Killer Whale headdress and the button blanket from Kwakwa̱ka̱'wakw lineage property to exotic non-Indigenous costume.[3] Thornton wrote that the "Indians of western Canada . . . provided romantic and

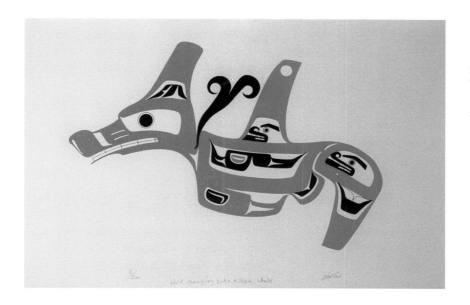

Figure 8. Tsaqwasupp Art Thompson (Nuu-chah-nulth), *Wolf Turning into a Killer Whale*, serigraph, 1979. RBCM 16262.

everything is one, and the understanding that the border between natural and supernatural worlds is porous and that beings can transform from one state to another. The orca/wolf transformation indicates orcas' connections to nuučaanuł cultural practice and knowledge. Supernal Wolves play an important role in nuučaanuł ceremonialism and teaching, and as whalers themselves, the nuučaanuł identify with orcas as hunters of whales.[6]

Indigenous accounts tell that people, too, can enter the ocean and be transformed into killer whales. A well-known Haida account concerns Nanasimget, whose wife was kidnapped by a killer whale and who travelled to the undersea world to rescue her. A simplified version of the story was published in a popular book by Hilary Stewart,[7] while a Kwakwa̱ka̱'wakw version was told and illustrated by Charlie

George from Blunden Harbour when he was a young patient of Dr. Richard Whitfield Large at the Bella Bella Hospital in the early twentieth century.[8] The story tells of Soogwilis, a chief of Blunden Harbour. His wife, Klaquaek (who was the daughter of a Wuikinuxv chief from Rivers Inlet), dropped a white seal skin into the water when trying to wash it and was carried away by a killer whale to the whales' village under the sea. Soogwilis went out in a big canoe with helpers from his village and descended to the ocean floor by climbing down a long ladder they had made out of saplings. There he followed a road to the village of the killer whales and found Klaquaek sitting in the house of the chief of the whales. The killer whale chief laughed when Soogwilis demanded her return, saying that she was already his wife and was already developing a hunchback (that is, she was becoming a killer whale, with a dorsal fin).[9] Advised by a jellyfish to create a diversion, Soogwilis spilled water over the hot cooking stones, and under cover of the resulting steam was able to grasp Klaquaek and flee. The jellyfish blocked the path of the pursuing whales by humping his back, as jellyfish do when they swim. Soogwilis and Klaquaek then reached the canoe and returned to their village. All the rest of her life, Klaquaek had a hunch back, a reminder that she had almost transformed into a killer whale.

Other versions of this story have been published in various anthropological texts,[10] and I have come to know this story at a remove, not from Indigenous storytellers but through these fragmentary secondhand accounts and, more immediately for me, through works of art. Haida argillite carvings and serigraphs illustrate the story of Nanasimget (figs. 9 and 10), and Charlie George made colour

drawings to illustrate his story of Soogwilis (fig. 11). These artworks are themselves symbols, objects of beauty and mystery encapsulating a whole universe of thought about the natural world and the beings within it.

Just as works of art are only parts of whole complexes of tangible and intangible Indigenous cultures, the Nanasimget and Soogwilis stories as recounted and interpreted in English for non-Indigenous audiences are condensed versions of much longer epics full of complex meanings. One of these appears in this book as *The Two Brothers at Tiiaan*, told in Haida by Chief 'Láanaas Sdang Adam Bell and translated by HIGáawangdlii Skilaa Lawrence Bell/ Gulḵiihlgad Marianne Boelscher Ignace (pages 52–60). It is a much more complete and nuanced telling of a short narrative that John R. Swanton included in *Contributions to the Ethnology of the Haida*:

Figure 9. Haida argillite pipe, nineteenth century. RBCM 16804.

Figure 10. Skil Kew Wat Freda Diesing (Haida Eagle Clan), *Scana with the Woman*, serigraph, 1980. RBCM 16859.

Figure 11. Charlie George (Kwakwaka'wakw), *Klaquaek Kidnapped by the Whale*, undated but 1900–1910. RBCM 15863.

a central concept for a maritime culture where the possibility of drowning was a fact of life.[12] These stories about killer whales tell of survival, death and transition between human and supernatural worlds.[13]

Two brothers went hunting buffleheads, and wounded one. Then they were invited under the sea, and entered the house of a Killer-Whale. There the eldest was transformed into a whale, like the others, but the youngest escaped. After he reached home again, his spirit was in the habit of going hunting with his elder brother, while his body remained in the house. In the morning his parents always found a black whale on the beach. One morning, however, the younger brother wept, declaring that his elder brother had been killed at Cape St James, and he had brought his body home. Going outside, they found the body of a Killer-Whale, and they built a grave-house for it.[11]

Adam Bell's full accounting of this story makes it clear that those lost at sea were thought to be transformed into killer whales,

John R. Swanton titled his version of the two brothers at Tiiaan story "How the Killer-Whale First Came to Be Used as a Crest." Killer Whale is a primary crest of the Haida Raven lineages (according to Swanton, it is the oldest of the Haida crests) and a major crest in all other Northwest Coast cultures as well, appearing on poles, house fronts, painted and carved screens, robes, headdresses, hats and other regalia, bracelets and jewellery, tattoos, storage boxes, spoons and more. A crest is an identifying design and may be a memorial to a supernatural encounter or ancestor, but it is more dynamic than that. As Marianne Boelscher Ignace points out, a crest is a "symbol of transaction" that symbolizes a complex, ongoing history of interpersonal and interlineage relationships for those who can interpret it.[14] But while the role of a crest as a symbol of the owner's wealth and history may be readable in some museum objects and catalogues, its

Figure 12. Mrs. Sam Hunt (Kwakwa̱ka̱'wakw), button blanket made about 1897. RBCM 12853.

crests enact. But I've seen no in situ historical photographs of a Kwakwa̱ka̱'wakw button blanket made about 1897 by Mrs. Sam Hunt (fig. 12), and while I can discern the Killer Whale crest designs and see how they would wrap around the body and refer to the wearer's identity, the lineage interactions and complex personal relationships that the crest represents did not travel with the blanket when it was purchased for the museum, about 70 years after it was made, and are beyond my personal knowledge.

transactional role is rarely captured. Museum documentation is a kind of conceptual palimpsest that overwrites original Indigenous meanings with new meanings structured by anthropological or colonial concepts. Sometimes the original cultural contexts are obliterated through this process; sometimes traces remain. Like the oral histories, crest images can have multiple versions and various meanings. Not all killer whale images can be readily understood by those unable to see and interpret the traces of cultural meaning.

Looking at the photographs of Chief Lagius's tunic and Charles Nowell's button blanket, for example, I am able to recognize the Killer Whales shown on them in profile, their blowing represented by lines from the blowholes, and from the photographs I have some idea of the relationships these

The Killer Whale fin that tops the Lagius-Nowell headdress has a hole in it, and it splits into two fins at the top, suggesting that the being represented is a special form or incarnation of the killer whale. Such unnaturalistic representations of orcas are common in crest art from throughout the Northwest Coast. They personify the equation of killer whales with power and supernatural beings made clear by the Haida word for killer whale, which can mean all of these.[15] Killer Whale fins with holes in them are a common motif (fig. 13), and there are also representations of Killer Whales with multiple fins (fig. 14). These may indicate particular crests, but they also have an underlying

Figure 13. Heiltsuk Killer Whale fin, part of an item of regalia now lost, collected by Bernard Filip Jacobsen in 1893 with no information. RBCM 54.

naturalness, with the multiple fins evoking a pod of whales swimming together.[16] The mix of natural and supernatural is discernable on a carving of a two-finned Killer Whale collected by James Deans in Haida Gwaii in 1892, described by Deans as a "model memorial crest" (fig. 15). The two-finned Killer Whale has a seal-like animal in its fearsome teeth. Since seals are a food of the orcas of the oceans around Haida Gwaii, this small detail attests to the presence of the supernatural being in the natural world. But whose crest this might be and why it takes the form it does has been completely overwritten by Deans'

agency and his minimal, archaizing description.[17]

A very old Haida crest hat in the museum collection is a palimpsest that works both ways (fig. 16). In this case a woolen cap—perhaps of the sort worn by European sailors or military men; its origin is unclear—was overwritten with an Indigenous interpretation. The addition of abalone eyes, beaded details of mouth and face, and a wooden fin with a hole in it and a face in its base has turned the hat into a Killer Whale headdress. It was collected by Newton Henry Chittenden in Haida Gwaii in 1884 with no information. Without its

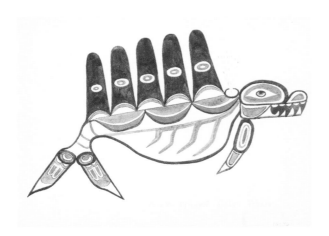

Figure 14. Kwakwa̱ka̱'wakw drawing (sketchbook page) of a five-finned Killer Whale. RBCM 19574.

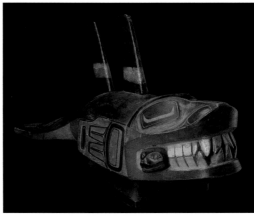

Figure 15. Haida carving collected in Haida Gwaii, 1892, by James Deans, who described it as a "model memorial crest." RBCM 237.

Figure 16. Haida "dance hat" collected by Newton Henry Chittenden in Haida Gwaii, 1884. RBCM 41.

connection to both sides of its origin, Indigenous and non-Indigenous, this intriguing object is mysterious and otherworldly. It is perhaps an example of the deliberate ambiguity of some crests, a characteristic that makes possible their movement between families and places. Crests that could symbolize more than one identity throughout their lifespan would support the concept, articulated by Boelscher (1988), that as symbols, crests are always being renegotiated, creating and validating social structures. They function within a system of relationships between people, and those human relationships in turn structure an understanding of the natural and supernatural worlds symbolically embodied in crest objects such as those that depict killer whales.

In Indigenous thought, glimpsed through representations of killer whales, orcas and people are analogous in symbolic ways. Colin Browne has written that "the ability to identify the ways in which one thing is analogous to another, or to its contrary, is at the heart of being—and all poetry and art—and will be critical to our survival."[18] Killer whales are the symbolic bridge between land and sea, able to travel between the two realms and connect people to all the inhabitants of the ocean. In their undersea villages, killer whales take off their whale cloaks and become like people. Sometimes people are taken to the killer whales' villages and become themselves killer whales. These stories are not just about a relationship between people and orcas; they are about enacting a relationship that has to be maintained, acknowledged and seen. The oral teachings are part of the great epics about the formation and nature of the world that have been recounted for millennia and are still told and learned from today. As transcribed by anthropologists such as John R. Swanton and told by elders such as Adam Bell, they are evocative, profound, timeless—and to non-Indigenous readers, enigmatic—accounts of the nature of the world and how to live in it. As industrialized societies face the ecological devastation they have caused and its consequences, these stories are important reminders that the earth and its oceans need to be understood and treated differently. The lessons they hold may indeed be critical to our survival and the survival of the orcas, who are, in Indigenous thought, our relatives. ➳

Notes

1 The painting is titled *Chief Charley Nowell*. Probably at the same time and place, Thornton also painted Chief Herbert Johnson wearing what appears to be the same blanket. Both portraits were reproduced, with the captions reversed, in *Potlatch People: Indian Lives and Legends of British Columbia*, a 2003 republication of Thornton's *Indian Lives and Legends* (1966).

2 The painting is RBCM 16499.

3 This is not the only photograph of Thornton in Indigenous costume. For example, a picture of her wearing a buckskin outfit, circa 1938, appears in a 1985 catalogue for a Thornton exhibition at the Butler Galleries, Vancouver.

4 Thornton, *Potlatch People*, *Indian Lives and Legends of British Columbia* (Surrey, BC: Hancock House, 2003).

5 The concept that wolves transform into orcas and orcas can become wolves as they move from land to sea is shared by other Indigenous groups, including the Yupik of Alaska.

6 Alan D. MacMillan, "Non-Human Whalers in Nuu-chah-nulth Art and Ritual: Reappraising Orca in Archaeological Context." *Cambridge Archaeological Journal* 29, no. 2 (May 2019).

7 Hilary Stewart, *Looking at Totem Poles* (Vancouver: Douglas & McIntyre, 1993), 42.

8 Large published the story and the drawings that illustrate it in *Soogwilis: A Collection of Kwakiutl Indian Designs & Legends* (Toronto: Ryerson, 1951).

9 In the Nanasimget story, she is being fitted with a carved killer whale fin.

10 A list compiled by Franz Boas includes references to versions recorded by Boas himself, James Deans, Charles Hill-Tout, Livingston Farrand, Aurel Krause and John R. Swanton. *Tsimshian Mythology* (Washington, DC: Smithsonian Institution, 1909–1910), 835, 840–42.

11 John R. Swanton, *Contributions to the Ethnology of the Haida* (New York: American Museum of Natural History, 1905), 231–32.

12 Marianne Boelscher, *The Curtain Within: Haida Social and Mythical Discourse* (Vancouver: UBC Press, 1988), 183.

13 George M. Dawson, *Report on the Queen Charlotte Islands*, Geological Survey of Canada Report on Progress for 1878–79 (Montreal: Dawson Brothers, 1880), 152b.

14 Boelscher, *Curtain*, 1988, 150.

15 Boelscher, *Curtain*, 1988, 160.

16 Thanks to Michael Nicoll Yahgulanaas for this observation.

17 Deans, a retired Hudson's Bay Company employee with an interest in Indigenous cultures, was the author of *Tales from the Totems of the Hidery*. This model is one of several in the Royal BC Museum that were collected, and likely commissioned, by Deans in 1889, all apparently intended as symbols of an exotic culture.

18 Colin Browne, *Entering Time: The Fungus Man Platters of Charles Edenshaw* (Vancouver: Talonbooks, 2016), 112.

The Two Brothers at Tiiaan

AS TOLD BY

Chief 'Láanaas Sdang Adam Bell of the Massett Haida, G̱aw Yahgu 'Láanaas clan

TRANSLATED BY **HlG̱áawangdlii Skilaa Lawrence Bell and Gulḵiihlgad Marianne Ignace**[1]

THIS GYÁAHLANG.EE[2] (clan narrative) was 'Láanaas Sdang's favourite
story. We recorded it with him during the summer of 1983 in two
nearly identical tellings. 'Láanaas Sdang (1902–1987) was the last trained
storyteller among the G̱aw X̱aadee (Massett Haida) and was the hereditary
chief of the G̱aw Yahgu 'Láanaas clan of the Massett Haida. At a potlatch
given in about 1913 or 1914, during the height of the anti-potlatch legislation, he succeeded his maternal great-uncle Xilaa as chief, his mother
having been appointed caretaker chief at the advice of Massett elders and
chiefs following Xilaa's death. The story of the two brothers is the first of
a cycle of four stories from Tiiaan, an ancestral Haida village on the west
coast of Graham Island once owned by the Dúu Git'ans Eagle clan. 'Láanaas
Sdang likely learned the Tiiaan stories from his father, Gid X̱iigans Phillip
Bell of the Ts'aahl 'Láanaas Eagles.

The two brothers' story speaks to Haida perceptions of, and interactions with, sG̱áan, killerwhales, the most powerful of ocean beings. In the
Haida way of thinking, feeling and being, they are the embodied souls of
humans who drowned at sea. As a fisherman all his life, 'Láanaas Sdang
had one or more near-death drowning experiences and had deep respect
and affinity for killerwhales. This is a story about the incomplete transformation of a young boy as punishment for having violated the Haida law
of respecting and not hurting animals—in this case the small bufflehead

(*Previous spread*) **THE RUNAWAYS** **KYLER VOS**

Pod T109A outside Clayoquot Sound, in front of Bartlett Island, July 12, 2017.

Bufflehead in Fanny Bay, BC, 2006. Jukka Jantunen photo.

ducks who are considered the "servants" or junior household members of killerwhales. The association is evoked by the killerwhale-like black and white markings of buffleheads, and the perception that they give birth to live offspring, just like humans and killerwhales. The story gives us vivid imagery of killerwhales as living in human-like dwellings and social arrangements beneath the ocean, and it evokes the role of the skin (k̲ál) as the medium of transformation. Although not transformed, but having been in the realm of killerwhales, the younger brother in the story needs to reclaim his humanity by washing off his killerwhale skin with fresh water. By having been exposed to the realm of killerwhales, he stays in communion with his older brother who was successfully transformed, hunting with him while his family sees him in a trance-like state sitting in the house. The story—although this is only briefly mentioned in the ending presented by 'Láanaas Sdang here—ends with the younger brother having to succeed his older brother after the latter gets killed in a war with killerwhales from Née Kún (Rose Spit). The law of matrilineal succession is stronger than the human desire to be among humans, and in the end he has no choice but to succeed his older brother. ∼⋗

~~~~~

Tiiaan 'lngee Gawdáasii dluu Gaa xadalaa ḵ'ask'ud ahl náanggaangaan.
'Wáagyaan nang sGwáan xyee 'l k'at'awGwáangaasii dluu,
dlaa 'l tluuḵáaydwaas gyáanaan,
'láa ga yáanang.eehlaawaan.
'Wáagyaan Tiiaan ḵ'adguu ḵadl ii'waan is, gu 'l Gidatl'aawasii dluu, gam tliijaan dluu
Gáayuu tl' gudáng'waa'anggaangaan.
Gam tliijaan 'l iswaas an 'l únsad'wa'angaan.
'Wáadluu 'l tsaan gu 'l … … [*pauses*], k'uu gyáat'aad 'l t'adwaas,
áajii xangii sda 'l ḵin(g)tl'aasii dluu, áajii k'áay giihlḵ'uhlgangs
gu k'áal xajuu giitl'aagreengaas.
Gu 'l ants'a(d)tl'aas dluu, "nang íitl'aagadaas uu daláng ists'aalgaa!"
'Wáagyaan háwsan 'l gíiyid'la'aan.
'Wáagyaan nang k'wáayaas uu isdagudáangaanii,
"Hl ḵáagahls dluu, gam Hl sdíihltl'aaxansgads dluu díi dlaa dáa hánsan ḵáagahl!"
hin uu dúunan(g) 'l súudaayaan.
'Wáagyaan 'l k'wáay ḵáagahlsdlaas gyaan 'l sGáyhl ḵáawd uu.
Jíingeehls dluu 'laa asan ḵáagahlsdlaayaan.
Áajii sda k'yuwée tl'iiwaas áahljii ing.gu 'l t'at'ahldlaas, 'l ḵáats'aayaan.
Née ii'wanG usdlee tiiwdaa ḵ'iw aa 'l ḵáatl'aas.
Gu 'l gyaans daan uu, 'l k'wáay anáa is an 'l unsadee uu.
'Láa tl' duutl'áawaas dluu, ga xaldangaas 'láa an duutl'aa'waas,
"nang iitl'aagadaas dáng ḵáats'aalgang."
'L ḵáats'aas dluu, 'l k'wáay ts'áanuwee stl'uudaasii aa 'l sgwáandawaas,
'Wáadluu áajii sGáanee, ts'iil hin uu t'aláng kya'áadang, áhljii 'láa an tl' xulk'íindaas
tl' kitl'a'aayaan ahlaa.
Ahl 'laa tl' kitl'a'aas, 'l k'wáay ḵ'áawaas sgwaayang Gii t'apsgadee hin uu áajii 'waa ga
isii, 'wáagyaan tl' gudangée 'láaGusdlaas,
"'laa hl isdagudánguu, 'laa hl isdagudánguu, kún.gadee sda 'laa hl Galḵáaḵ'ahluu!
Kún.gadee sda 'l Galḵáak'ahlwaayaan.
'Wáagyaan kún.gadee sda 'laa 'l Gálḵáak'ahls dluu, "áajii tangee kwahGajaasii hl
ḵínggang," hin 'l sáawaan.
'Wáagyaan 'l k'wáay kwahtl'aasiis 'l gudángaawaan.
'Wáagyaan 'l k'wáay sda Gidatl'awaagaan,
'wáagyaan 'láa hansan tl' isdeeds.
'Wáagyaan áajii tl'ak'ee 'l ḵánxagangs,

~~~~~~~

While there was a town at Tiiaan,[3] children were playing with buffleheads, so they say.
And they broke the wing of one of them by hitting it with a rock,
and after they set out to paddle after it in their canoes,
fog came upon them, they say.
There is a big reef out from Tiiaan, and as they arrived there,
they could not hear any surf at all.
And they were clueless about where they were.
And then, while on the ocean, they were wearing marten blankets, they peeked through the eye-holes
in their blankets, and in a hairy, tangled-up ball of kelp on the surface they saw a little sculpin
surfacing in the green of the ocean.
As it surfaced its head above the water there, [it said] "The chief orders you to come in!"
And it went back down under, floating away.
And the older brother wanted to try it out.
"After I go in, if I don't come back after awhile, you too, go in!"
This is what he said to his younger brother.
And he (younger brother) cried for awhile after his older brother had gone under.
After a long time, he also went in.
And he stepped onto what was a ladder hanging from there, and he entered [the ocean].
When he climbed down he came upon the front of a really big longhouse.
While he was standing there, he realized his brother was inside.
They came out to get him; the slaves came out to get him, [saying],
"The chief invites you in!"
When he entered, he saw his older brother standing by the embers of the fire, warming his back.
And this killerwhale dorsal fin, we call it ts'iil, they were heating it up for him,
to shove it into him.
When they had stabbed him with it, it got wedged inside the sitting older brother's back,
and it stayed wedged, and they were happy.
"Try him out, try him out, lead him out of the corner!" [i.e., give him a test run].
They led him out of the corner.
As they led him towards where the water was flowing, one of them said,
"I can see the water flowing out fast."
They could hear the older brother blowing like a whale as he was going out.
And from the older brother having arrived outside [i.e., succeeded in his transformation],
now they started the process with the younger brother.
As they were trying to pierce him [with the fin] he flung the whetstone

sgwaa'ang gwii 'l k'aat'ee uu ahl 'láa tl' kitgee dluu,

'láa sda hingaan G̱asG̱asgads, daa.ee G̱ii t'ap'sgads,

háwsan 'láa G̱idée tl' ḵaawgáa ḵáawd uu, ḵánang gu tl' isdee 'láa tl' gulaas dluu, áasgee
kihlyaagahls, áasgee gu tl'aa uu áajii tl'ak'aa angaa 'l xuywáasiis,

'Wáa hingaan ahl 'láa tl' kidgee, háwsan íijaanee gingaan, háwsan 'láa tl' G̱asG̱asgadée,
dáa.ee G̱ii t'ap'sgadée 'wáa ga híildangs.

'Wáadluu hawsan 'laa G̱adee tl' ḵaawgáa ḵáawd uu, 'l duulee áasgee gu kihlyáagahls
dluu, áasgee sda 'láa tl' isdagudánghangḵasaayaan.

Stansanggee gu 'laa tl' isdagudángs dluu, nang íitl'aagadaas uu gudáa'angaayaan,

'Láa hl ḵáakhlaadáa-uu, 'láa hl ḵáakhlaadáa-uu."

"HlG̱an ga 'l gwaawaang," hin uu 'l saawaan,

"hlG̱an ga 'l gwaawaang."

'Wáagyaan 'lngee gu tl' ḵáa'ungwaangs dluu, tl' isdaalgangs dluu,

gam nang tl' 'láa ga ḵéeyaa'anggaangaan.

'Wáadluuwaan 'láa gu nang ḵáatl'aas dluu, "gasantl'aa uu tlíijee dáng is'gwaanggaa?"

hin uu 'láa 'l súudaayaan.

"Gam tlíijaan x̱aadlaa k'yuwée ga an díi unsada'angs dluu,

ahljii ahluu áa Hl íijang."

"haay, áadsgwaa 'lngee kún gu nang uu nawaas, 'lngee gyáa gu nang nawaas aa hl ḵáa.

'Wáagyaan 'láa aa hl ḵáa, nang ḵ'iiyaas uu iijang, 'láa hl kyáanang,

'wáadluu áa hl nawaas duulii yaa

hl ḵáak'ahl!

Húu k'yuwée íijaa. Tiiaan 'lngee yahgu tajgwáa sG̱áan G̱ándlaas xyaangs duulaa

ḵwaa ii'wans ḵ'iiwdaa. Ts'ilaak'uu hin uu 'l kya'áang.

Áatl'an yaa uu dáng ḵáatl'agalaaḵasaang. Áatl'an yaa uu dáng kaatl'agal'saang.

'Wáadluu 'l awlang sG̱áygadaas,

'l ḵáats'aas dluu k'yuwée 'waa ga 'l ḵáak'udsii, 'l ḵáak'udsii.

'L awlang gud x̱anhlaas ga ándaas,

hin 'láa G̱adée agan an 'l dadlhlaas dluu,

"Áajii sḵal 'láagaangs," hin uu nang awáas, nang hánsan,

"jáa, díi asan sḵal gudánggang!"

'L aw 'láa G̱adee 'l'gid an dadlhlaas uu 'l áandanggaangaan.

'Wáagyaan tlíisdluuwaan uu G̱agwii uu 'l sG̱áyhliid daan,

'l sG̱áyhliidee dalée asan gu'úuwG̱usdlaas

'Wáagyaan áajii née kún.gadaa sda G̱ándlee ḵwah hlgiijúusii, 'l ḵingsii

"wáagyaan, "áajii x̱id guu hl ḵ'áawshlangaas dluu 'láahlangaa?" hin 'l gudáangaan.

Áa 'l ḵáas gyaan gu ''l ḵ'aawaan,

that he wore on his chest onto his back.

Thus, [instead of sticking to his back], it bounced off him and got wedged in the steps of the housepit.

And again, they talked about it for a while, and they decided to put it [the fin] on his chest,
but he had already flung his whetstone there.

And when they stabbed him again with it [the dorsal fin], it went the same way as before;
it ricocheted off him again and got wedged in the steps, where it moved, quivering.

And again, they talked about him for a while, and agreed⁴ to stab him in the side, and that's what
they came to an agreement about, that is what they figured they would do with him.

When they were on their fourth attempt, the chief reconsidered what they were doing:
"Let him go out, let him go out."

He is refusing the fin. That's what they said, "He's refusing the fin"
[i.e., he doesn't want to be transformed into an underwater supernatural being].

Then he was walking around the village, but he was not visible
to humans walking around.

And then, he came into appearance [became visible] to this one person, who said to him,
"What are you doing walking around here?"⁵

"I don't know where the people's trail is,
that is why I am here."

"Well, go to the point [at the end of] the village, there is a certain one living there. Where someone lives
next to the village, go to him. There is an old person living there, you ask him."

[The old man, when he got there, said to him]
"Beside where I live, you walk straight up towards the woods."

That's where there is a trail. Right in the front centre of Tiiaan flows Killerwhale Spring,
beside it is a big rock, it's called Ts'iilaak'uu.

And right there is where you will come ashore. Right there is where you will come ashore."⁶

And his mothers [and aunties, i.e., the women of his clan] were crying about him.

When he entered [their house], he slammed the door shut, he slammed it shut.

His mother and aunties were sitting shoulder to shoulder, huddled together.

As they were sitting huddled together, and as he wedged himself between them,
one of the aunties felt a sensation, "I have this twitching sensation in my shoulder," she said, and
another one said, "Yes, I also can 'hear' it with my shoulder!" [i.e., they sensed something].

His mother felt it when her child wedged himself between them.

After a long time, he finally started to cry [because he was still invisible to them].

When he cried, the rain started to fall heavily,
and he saw the rainwater pouring down from the corner of the house,
and he wondered, "Would it be good if I sat down under this?"

And he went there and sat down.

'Wáadluu Gándlee 'l ḵaj gwii kwah.hlgíijúusii
áasii dluu 'l tadáa sda 'l dlasdlaas dluu, sda 'l gya'áagaan
'l gya'áasii dluu, 'wáajii sǴáanee ḵ'ál 'láa sda Ǵatl'adguustlaayaan
Tlaan 'l sǴáyhlas dluu dalée asan tlaan gu'úuwaayaan.
'Wáagyaan 'l jaas ḵáatl'aawaas dluu dáa'ang 'l ḵéengaan.
"akyáa díi dáa ḵ'áawaang," hingaan tl'aa uu 'l aw 'l sgiḵ'ang.gaang.aan, 'láa 'l sgidaan.
Haws tlaan 'l suus gyaan 'l kil yank'yaan 'láa . . . .
Gam tlaan, gam 'l ḵayánsdlaas, akyaa tl' ḵíngwaas gyaan
akyaa 'l dáa ḵ'aawaayaan.
Akyáa 'l dáa ḵ'aawaas damáan 'l ḵings dluu, 'láa tl' ḵáats'adaayaan.
Áasgee sduu jíingaa awlang ḵ'uhl 'l íijaan.
Hawáan Ǵiidan daan uu 'l hlkwiidasdlaayaan.
"díi k'wáay uu díi taantl'aagaang sáayee an aa"
'Wáajii Ǵiid kihlaalwee 'láa Ǵaduu 'l gíihlals,
Ǵáalee 'l stlee Ǵii 'laagahl l' sḵ'asdlee uu, 'l k'ut'ahl.
'Wáadluwaan sáandlaans dluu 'l ḵats'ee 'l kwahsaas 'láa tl' gudángaan.
'láa tl' duu xúusdlaas gyaan,
"áadsgwaa uu díi k'wáay díi t'aang.ad gyaan huu áadsgwaa uu 'l iijang."
Áajii ḵaayee gud Ǵaads ḵ'iidlts'aasii, 'láa ga'lngee ga tl' isdaas
damáan gin ga halée 'l guuláaǴusdlaawaasii
Gu 'l is uu. . . . Táa uu, 'lngee xáadee Ǵan 'l ḵ'íihlangee ḵáawd uu
Née Kún Ǵaa asan 'l k'wáay gud 'l ḵáawsdlaayaan,
Née Kún.gee gu sǴáan uu Ḵ'aa Kún hin uu 'l kya'aadang.
Áasgee gu 'l istl'aawaas dluu, 'l k'wáay gam tl' guuláa'angs
aganaan uu 'l k'wáay tl' tiiyaayaan.
'Wáagyaan 'l k'wáay ḵ'ud 'l Ǵidatl'aadaasii dluu,
'láa Ǵadée tl' guusuu ḵaawd uu,
Ǵii tl' k'ananángs gyaan, Ǵud Ǵii 'láa tl' isdaayaas gyaan
Sáahlang xáad hin uu tl' kya'áadaang,
áahlguusd Ǵii uu 'láa tl' isdaayaan.
Tlii sǴáan 'yaadgaas hak'un tl' isdadlásdlaayaan,
'Wáagyaan nang dúunaas iitl'aagadeelaan, 'l sǴáaneelan.
Ahljii ahluu áayaad hawaan sǴáanee iitl' kil gudánggang.
Ahljii ahluu áa sǴáan giits'aad hin uu áajii xiṯiid, ḵ'ask'ud, hin uu kyee jahlii Ǵiidang.
SǴáan giits'aad uu Ǵid.
Áa uu Ǵusdlagee, gadée!

And there, the water splashed down on his head,
his whole body got cold, and he stood up from there.
While he stood there, that killerwhale skin flopped off him, wet and heavy.
When he stopped crying, the rain stopped falling.
When his sister stepped out of the house, she saw her brother.[7]
"My brother is sitting outside!" But instead, her mother spanked her into crying, she spanked her.[8]
She wouldn't stop talking, she carried on…
When she didn't stop, and she didn't give up [talking about her brother sitting outside], they looked
outside and they saw the brother sitting there.
Her brother was sitting outside, and when they saw him, they told him to come in.
From there, he stayed with his mother's clan for a long time.
By and by, he got worried (excited).
"It is because my older brother is coming to get me to go hunting."
And they placed hunting weapons on him, fastening them to his belt.
They put a paddle in his hand, he was [like] dead [i.e., was in a trance-like state].
In the morning they could hear him blowing like a killerwhale as he entered the house.
After everyone rushed to get him, [he would say],
"Over there is my older brother, my steersman, on the beach."
This sealion [they had hunted], they gave half of it to the village.
They really enjoyed going after them [the sealions, on their hunting trips].
For awhile they got lots of food for the townspeople.
And his older brother wanted to go to Née Kún.
(The killerwhales called Née Kún Ḵ'aa Kún.)
And when they got there, they didn't like older brother,
and so they killed the older brother.
And when they arrived with the dead body of older brother [i.e., a killerwhale body],
they talked about it for a while,
they cut him up into pieces, and placed him in a box,
(we call it a mortuary pole [or burial box])
and that is where they put him.
They put the whole body of the killerwhale inside [of the burial container].
And younger brother had to succeed him as chief, he became a killerwhale.
And so even today the killerwhales understand our speech.
And that is why these little birds, the buffleheads, that is what their real name is,
they are the killerwhales' servants.[9]
It's really like that, precious one!

Notes

1 Chief 'Láanaas Sdang Adam Bell recounted the story in Vancouver in 1983. Marianne Boelscher Ignace and Lawrence Bell translated it in 1985 and transcribed it in 2012. Claude Jones checked the text in 2014. It was reviewed by Ignace and Bell in 2017.

2 We are grateful to Marianne Boelscher Ignace and Lawrence Bell, son of Chief Adam Bell, for permission to publish this Haida account. It is a more complete and accurate version of an oral tradition that John R. Swanton heard in Haida Gwaii in 1900 or 1901 and published in *Contributions to the Ethnology of the Haida* (1905: 231–232). See Martha Black's essay in this book (pages 36–49).

3 For information about Tiiaan and its history, see George MacDonald, *Haida Monumental Art: Villages of the Queen Charlotte Islands* (Vancouver: UBC Press), pages 204–205.

4 The Haida term is literally to "straighten out words."

5 The man who implies that the younger brother belongs out in the ocean must be a sG̲aagaa, or medicine man, who can see him walking around in a killerwhale skin, invisible to other humans.

6 "Coming ashore" here is used metaphorically, meaning "this is where you will enter the human world."

7 After the rain has washed off his killerwhale skin, the boy becomes visible to normal humans.

8 This is a very Haida sentence: using the spanking as an instrument to cause crying.

9 Giits'aad are not slaves, but younger male household members who follow the orders of their maternal uncle, who would have been a clan or house chief, but they were also under the protectorship of the uncle or chief.

Killer Whales of the Southern Hemisphere

Jared Towers and Rebecca Wellard

THE KILLER WHALE is the apex marine predator. It preys on a wide range of species throughout the world's oceans, making it one of the most ecologically diverse and widespread species on the planet. Several types of killer whale exist, and culturally distinct high-latitude populations that typically exploit different prey resources are referred to as *ecotypes*. In the Southern Hemisphere at least five ecotypes can be readily distinguished by their dramatically different appearances and behavioural characteristics. Although these physically and ecologically unique types of killer whale often occur in the same area at the same time, they rarely, if ever, socialize, and genetic evidence indicates that some populations haven't interbred for hundreds of generations. This multi-component divergence is indicative of a species complex that may warrant recognition of several distinct species or sub-species within the genus *Orcinus*.

The most striking type of killer whale in the Southern Hemisphere may also be the largest and most widespread. It is jet black and white, with a slanted forehead and a medium-sized eye patch. Males and females measure up to 9 and 7.7 metres in length, respectively, and the dorsal fins and flippers of adult males are about a metre longer than those of adult females. In the waters south of the Polar Front, including those around Antarctica, this form of killer whale is referred to as type A.

Type A killer whales are best known for preying on minke whales and elephant seals around the Antarctic Peninsula, but they also eat other small whales and pinnipeds. Like most mammal-eating killer whales in other regions, type A killer whales typically travel in small groups of four to eight individuals that hunt spread out over several hundred metres and presumably maintain acoustic silence in order not to alert their prey. This small group size probably helps to ensure that hunts are efficient and that

An adult female type A killer whale surfaces near the Antarctic Peninsula, 2019. Note the two dark circular scars from cookie-cutter shark bites on her saddle patch. Jared Towers photo.

each individual can maximize energy intake when a kill is made. However, type A killer whales are also occasionally known to form large groups. For example, on a recent research expedition to Antarctica, we recorded a highly vocal group of 28 type A killer whales that later caught and consumed a large pinniped, likely an elephant seal.

Some type A killer whales tagged near the Antarctic Peninsula have been found to travel north of the Polar Front into the South Pacific and South Atlantic Oceans, and small, circular cookie-cutter shark scars on the bodies of others indicate that they make trips to warm pelagic waters. These whales may be part of a large breeding population or constitute one of several distinct killer whale populations found throughout the Southern Hemisphere, all with similar behaviours and appearance. For example, there are killer whales

indistinguishable from type A whales in the subantarctic to warm temperate waters of the South Atlantic, South Pacific and Indian Oceans, and the more research is conducted, the more it appears that their diets are similarly diverse.

In the Falkland Islands and the Prince Edward Islands of the Indian Ocean, at Crozet Island, at Macquarie Island, and at Punta Norte, Argentina, small groups of killer whales are well known for seasonally patrolling coastal waters, where they take elephant seal pups that venture into the shallows off the beaches where they were born. But at Crozet Island, in the Prince Edward Islands and in Argentina, the same killer whales that have been documented eating seals have also been found eating fish. Other killer whales with varied diets are found in Australia and South Africa, where field observations and stomach contents analysis has revealed that some individuals prey on a mixture of cetaceans, pinnipeds, fishes and squid. For example, killer whales found off the coast of south-western Australia have been observed preying on squid, beaked whales and blue whales, and the stomach contents of some killer whales off South Africa included cetacean, fish and squid remains. Although any of these populations may rely on specific prey species at specific times, their overall generalist diets are interesting because in some regions, killer whales that eat mammals will not hunt fish, and those that eat fish will not hunt mammals.

By comparison, types B and C killer whales are very different from these and type A killer whales in a number of ways. The most obvious differences are that their dark pigment is charcoal grey, not black, and that their foreheads are more sharply slanted than type A killer whales. Type B and C killer whales also all have sharply defined curved lines running from the bottom of their saddle patches to the upper forward edges of their eye patches. This unique characteristic is referred to as a dorsal cape. These caped killer whales also share some other characteristics. For example, they are only known to feed south of the Polar Front, and because their skin cannot regenerate in such cold water, they are often completely covered in a growth of yellow diatoms. These whales make frequent migrations to warm water thousands of miles to the north, where they regenerate their skin and shed the diatoms, but they are often bitten by cookie-cutter sharks during these tropical excursions. Despite all the similarities between Bs and Cs, these forms also have significant differences from each other, and the more we learn about each of them, the more distinct each appears to be.

Type B killer whales have a circumpolar distribution around Antarctica, including South Georgia Island, and are easily recognized by their enormous eye patches. Some groups within the Antarctic Circle are known for travelling in small groups of four to twelve individuals and hunting seals,

predominantly Weddell seals, amongst the pack ice. These whales, commonly referred to as B1s or pack ice killer whales, use a dramatic hunting technique called "wave-washing," in which they all swim quickly along the surface towards an ice floe with a seal on it. They synchronously dive just before hitting it, and kick up a large wave with their flukes, which washes the seal off the ice. They are highly sexually dimorphic and can be quite large, some roughly the same size as type A individuals. Another type B killer whale found around the Antarctic Peninsula travels in much larger groups of 20 to more than 100 individuals, is less sexually dimorphic, and is up to a metre shorter than the B1s. These B2, or Gerlache, killer whales have been observed preying on penguins, although they likely also consume other small prey such as fish

Gerlache/type B killer whales chase a Gentoo penguin near the surface waters of the Gerlache Strait, Antarctica, 2017. Jared Towers photo.

An adult female and two juvenile Gerlache/type B killer whales surface in the Gerlache Strait, Antarctica, 2019. Note the large eyepatches, dorsal cape, and how their entire bodies are covered in yellow diatoms. Jared Towers photo.

or squid. Other type B killer whales found predominantly along the shelf edge around South Georgia Island are known to depredate Patagonian toothfish from commercial longline fishing vessels—an individual that we tagged in 2015 made the deepest dive known for a killer whale when it dove to 1,087 metres to steal toothfish off a longline. They usually travel in groups of 20 to 30. Acoustic studies on the call repertoire of type B killer whales in Antarctica include whistles, pulsed calls, and echolocation clicks similar to those reported from killer whales in other regions. Most calls of type B1 killer whales demonstrate a simple structure, with single-component calls dominating the repertoire, while type B2 killer whales demonstrate a higher number of multi-component calls and biphonations.

Type C killer whales, also known as Ross Sea killer whales, are currently the smallest form known, with the largest adult male measured at 6.1 metres. They have a narrow, slanted eye patch and are found mainly in eastern Antarctica, where they inhabit the inshore waters along the edge of the fast ice. They have been observed preying on large Antarctic tooth-

fish, but stable isotope analysis and field observations indicate they also consume lower trophic level prey such as small fish or squid. They have been commonly reported in McMurdo Sound for more than a century, and since the early 1970s they have taken advantage of foraging habitat made available when icebreakers create channels through the ice for supply ships to gain access to McMurdo Station. In this area, groups of 50 to 100 individuals have been recorded, analogous with large group sizes of fish-eating killer whales in other regions. However, these large aggregations may be in part due to the unique habitat of shifting ice floes and the requirement of numerous animals to all use the same breathing holes. Acoustic studies have revealed that type C killer whales produce many biphonations and complex calls with multiple frequency-modulated and pulsed components. This diverse and intricate call repertoire may reflect the feeding ecology and social structure of this type of killer whale.

The fifth and most poorly known killer whale in the Southern Hemisphere has been referred to as the type D or subantarctic killer whale. These whales are the familiar black and white, but with very blunt foreheads and remarkably tiny eye patches, less than one-tenth the size of those of type B killer whales. Their dorsal fins are pointier and more swept back than in any other killer whales, and although the dorsal fins of adult males are noticeably larger than those of adult females, both sexes appear to be similarly sized. They typically travel in large groups of 15 to 50 individuals and have been documented in cold temperate and subantarctic pelagic waters of the South Atlantic, South Pacific, Indian and Southern Oceans, primarily north of the Polar Front. The type D killer whale is well known for depredating Patagonian toothfish from commercial longline fishing vessels both at Crozet Island and off southwestern Chile. However, one juvenile that we recently filmed underwater off Chile had significant tooth wear, perhaps indicating a diet that includes sharks.

Killer whale ecology in the Southern Hemisphere is complex. Analysis to date demonstrates genetic diversity amongst types, and their different morphological and behavioural traits further highlight how divergent they are. Unique specializations related to diets, dialects, and other social behaviours are socially transmitted, indicating that these killer whale types are also culturally discrete. The degrees of divergence and convergence between killer whale cultures and the strength of reproductive isolation between types are topics that must be further investigated, as the forces driving killer whale evolution are unclear. Did

An adult male Subantarctic/type D killer whale surfaces off Cape Horn, Chile, 2019. Note the tiny eyepatch and blunt forehead. Jared Towers photo.

different types evolve due to resource competition, because of opportunities to exploit unique ecological niches, because of ancient geographic or ecological barriers, or because of a combination of these or other factors? In any case, the diversity amongst killer whale populations in the Southern Hemisphere has significant implications for taxonomy and conservation, as these populations highlight the significance of evolutionary ecology and raise questions about what level of divergence warrants classification and protection. Indeed, it may only be through understanding, classifying and conserving marine apex predators that we can gain a better appreciation for life in the ocean and how it survives. ～ン

Killer Whales

Ken Balcomb

THE COMMON ENGLISH NAME OF THE KILLER WHALE is applied to a group of top-predator marine mammals in the dolphin family, known since antiquity by reputation of their voracious appetite and cunning, group-organized, predatory lifestyle. Virtually any living animal of significant size in the sea could potentially be a meal for these savage beasts—or so it once seemed. That perception has changed rapidly in recent years, as populations of these majestic animals have become better known from field studies and molecular genetics. We now know that there are at least 10 potentially different species in the group we call killer whales, all of whom are descended from ancestral populations from the North Atlantic Ocean in the last million years. Known by different names in different languages and cultures, these strikingly impressive animals are now found in all oceans and seas worldwide. The killer whales of British Columbia, colloquially known as orcas, are indisputably the most studied of any in the world, but the cumulative result of all studies worldwide is painting a parallel picture to human evolution that we all might pause to appreciate. It is a big picture of all life on this planet we call Earth.

Humans are the indisputable ruling species on the land masses of Planet Earth, and killer whales are the indisputable top predators of the vast seas. We are each at the pinnacle of our respective domains. Humans, once totally terrestrial primates, are now capable of affecting the survival of all life in the sea, including its pinnacle species, through industrial marine activities and anthropogenic climate change. On the other hand,

(*Previous spread*) **BIGG'S ORCA ADRIEN MULLIN**

A female Bigg's orca hunts Pacific white-sided dolphins at the mouth of Kingcome Inlet, BC, August 2017.

A Southern Resident orca pod swimming together in Haro Strait, 2012. Ken Balcomb photo.

killer whales, as amazing as they are, cannot directly affect human domain of the land, representing an imbalance of the two most cerebral species the world has ever known. How did this happen in such a short time? And why? (We will leave the latter question for later.)

To begin with, we know that whales cannot swim through land; we also know that the water connection between the North Atlantic Ocean and the North Pacific Ocean via the Bering Strait has been clear only for brief periods of time during the interglacials, when there was a sufficient depth of water through which whales could swim. One of these interglacial warming periods is happening currently, one occurred about 120,000 years ago, and others occurred at approximately 100,000-year intervals through the Pleistocene epoch, which lasted 1.5 million years. Several times during the past million

Bigg's orca T37B pursues a sea lion in the Strait of Juan de Fuca, August 1, 2014. Ken Balcomb photo.

years there was enough water in the Bering Strait for the whales to swim through the passage. The rest of the time it was blocked by land and ice. The Bering Land Bridge theory suggests that around 70,000 years ago, anatomically modern humans trekked out of Africa and radiated over the land masses of Europe and Asia, reaching what is called the Bering Land Bridge, or Beringia, around 15,000 years ago. Their arrival was at the beginning of the current interglacial, when the ice retreated enough for them to walk from Siberia to North America before the sea rose to form the Bering Strait. Some of these humans then trekked through a valley between two great ice sheets, travelling as far as what is now Montana. From there, the genetic

evidence suggests that these early humans spread throughout all of North and South America from a founding population of perhaps fewer than 100 individuals.

The killer whales were already in the Pacific Northwest when the humans arrived, having swum through the Bering Strait during an earlier interglacial period. We surmise from the genetic distance between the so-called Resident killer whales of the Pacific Northwest and the North Atlantic fish-eating killer whales that this fish-eating Resident ecotype came through the Bering Strait approximately 120,000 years ago.

When we look at the genetic distance between the so-called Transient killer whales of the Pacific Northwest and the North Atlantic killer whales, we must conclude that the Transients came through much earlier, and they were and are very different beasts with a carnivorous diet. In all probability, these two ecotypes of killer whales will eventually be assigned separate species names, but for now they are all *Orcinus orca*, together with all of the other ecotypes of killer whales in the world. The ecotypes do not interbreed in nature, and they possess all the attributes of culture as we define it for humans: from generation to generation, they pass along behaviour patterns and communication modalities that are unique to each ecotype. Nonetheless, within the ecotypes all individuals are very family oriented, with distinct matrilines from which there is limited or no dispersal. Each matriline can grow more numerous in times of prolonged prey abundance, and over time each matriline must reach a limit of growth within the carrying capacity of its prey resource. Often several matrilines of an ecotype travel together, especially when prey resources are abundant in an area, such as in the Salish Sea. These killer whale aggregations are known as "pods" or "superpods." Dietary specialization and generalization, respectively, are quite a handy arrangement for the Residents and Transients in the Pacific Northwest, because they do not compete for food resources in nature and they both have free range of the same habitat. In fact, it could be said that the Transients help the Residents by reducing the other predator populations (like seals and sea lions) that come into the area in times of plenty and dine on fish that the Residents require.

A few basic facts apply to all killer whales:

1. Each whale must eat the equivalent of 2.5 to 5 per cent of its body weight per day, and for an average 3,600-kilogram whale, that equates to 90 to 180 kilograms of food per day! Although individuals can go prolonged times without food intake, they do so by metabolizing the blubber that provides both thermal insulation and energy storage for lean times. Some captive killer whales have been known to survive a month without food, but there are energetic and toxic costs for missing too many meals in the wild.

2. Sexual maturity occurs for both sexes by their teens, but males typically wait a few more years until social maturity before they mate. Mating is *not* monogamous and is almost always outside of the matriline.

3. Natural lifespan may extend from 80 to over 100 years for females and 60 years for males, but the average lifespan for Resident females is 54, and for Resident males, 29.

4. Normal full-term pregnancies last 17 to 18 months, and a newborn weighs about 180 kilograms and is between 1.8 and 2.4 metres long.

Southern Resident K25 breaches in Haro Strait, September 4, 2017. He would die of malnutrition in 2019. Ken Balcomb photo.

5. Males are typically larger than females by about 25 per cent at maturity.

6. In Pacific Northwest Resident populations of killer whales, the social structure is very strongly matrifocal as well as matrilineal (the mother is most important as a leader of the family, with even male offspring remaining with their mothers throughout their lives). In Pacific Northwest Transient populations, the young stay with their mother until sexual maturity, and then the males often disperse from the family (but not always). The female offspring of both ecotypes typically stay with their mother, or at least get together often.

All killer whales are travellers, easily swimming for 120 to 160 kilometres per day, and ranging over thousands of kilometres of ocean. Southern Resident killer whales used to be seen almost daily back and forth off Victoria during summer and autumn salmon spawning runs in the core area of southern entrances to the Salish Sea, and Northern Resident killer whales likewise frequented the northern entrances at Johnston Strait and Queen Charlotte Sound.

Young Bigg's orcas frolicking with double breach, May 17, 2015, near Yeo Point, Salt Spring Island, BC. Ken Balcomb photo.

Both Southern and Northern Resident killer whales specialize in consuming chinook salmon, the largest and most nutritious of five salmon species that formerly were fantastically abundant in the Pacific Northwest. These two BC killer whale Resident populations have rarely overlapped in time and place, and they have not interbred for many generations. It is often asked, "Why are the Northerns doing so much better than the Southerns?" The answer is simple: the returning, spawn-ready salmon are migrating from their northern feeding grounds in Alaska and the high-latitude North Pacific Ocean toward the rivers where they began life. They have to pass through a gauntlet of Alaska Resident and Northern Resident killer whales before they get to the southern range of rivers that the fish swim "home" to. The Southern Residents are the last in the foodline for salmon coming from the cold, productive northern waters to rivers in British Columbia and further south. Additionally, humans are also harvesting in this gauntlet, taking as much as 90 per cent of the fish, and there are simply not enough fish getting to the spawning beds in rivers to keep the natural ecosystem functioning. Even those fish that make it to the river's entrance may not make it to their spawning regions, due to in-river pollution, predators, overfishing, destruction of habitat and dams.

Killer whales and the humans migrated to and established their home range in the Pacific Northwest for the same reasons: here was an abundant, year-round stable food supply upon which top predators could survive and thrive.

With five species of anadromous salmon and hundreds of rivers and streams, each with a slightly different timing of seasonal water flow optimal for spawning conditions, there was almost always a run of salmon available somewhere in the neighbourhood. The major rivers of the region often had spawning runs of salmon numbering in the millions, allowing for huge human harvests of fish that were dried, smoked and preserved for future meals and for trade. The humans established their villages near these rivers and exchanged salmon with other humans for resources that were abundant elsewhere. It did not take long before the Indigenous people, who themselves were organized into extended families, noticed that the arrival of the killer whale families coincided with the arrival of the salmon, and it became established in mythology that the whales brought the salmon for the humans to eat. As in other anthropocentric belief systems, perhaps the whales were

J36 nudges her calf, J52, playfully in Haro Strait, BC, March 20, 2016. J52 died of malnutrition in 2019. Ken Balcomb photo.

Southern Resident killer whale in Haro Strait, BC, October 23, 2006, with J1 in the background. Ken Balcomb photo.

brother humans in the sea. The whales became spirit animals, along with raven, bear and eagle, to be revered with totems and celebrations of life in this Pacific Northwest land of plenty. Such a belief system is compatible with a scientific worldview in that it revealed the existence of a complex ecosystem in a way that worked for humans while acknowledging the role of the neighbouring animals and plants. For at least ten thousand years, the parallel existence of humans and killer whales in the Pacific Northwest worked well, as both dined upon the bountiful salmon that never stopped returning to the rivers and streams to spawn and die, bringing the nutrients that fed the forests and all of its creatures. And for a hundred thousand years before the humans arrived, the killer whales and the salmon co-evolved, creating and encouraging a nutrient flow from sea to mountaintop that we have been too slow to appreciate. We now know that much of the nitrogen in the trees of the forest is of marine origin, brought by the salmon from the sea.

Salmon and their supporting ecosystem are why everything was bountiful in the Pacific Northwest in the past. The bounty is now gone. Rivers are forever changed, spawning habitat is degraded, and salmon populations are dwindling. Over half of the salmon runs south of British Columbia are already extinct. The industrialization of western North America is the reason for this change.

The trees have been harvested, and the system is broken in many ways. At the very least, humans need to reduce their impact on coastal ecosystems and streams connected to the marine environment. We need to reduce salmon harvest and encourage restoration of natural runs. We need to restore nearshore habitat along the coast for herring, smelt and other fishes to support the marine phase of salmon life cycles. We need to restore salmon spawning habitat to prevent extinction of spawning runs under stress. And if generations of politicians commit to such a strategy, we may once again have salmon on the menu. Reducing our impact on the ecosystem is much easier than sending a rocket to the moon, but if we fail and salmon stocks go extinct, and if climate change runs wild thanks to our inability to self regulate, we may ourselves join the growing list of extinct species in the fossil record. ∼⤫

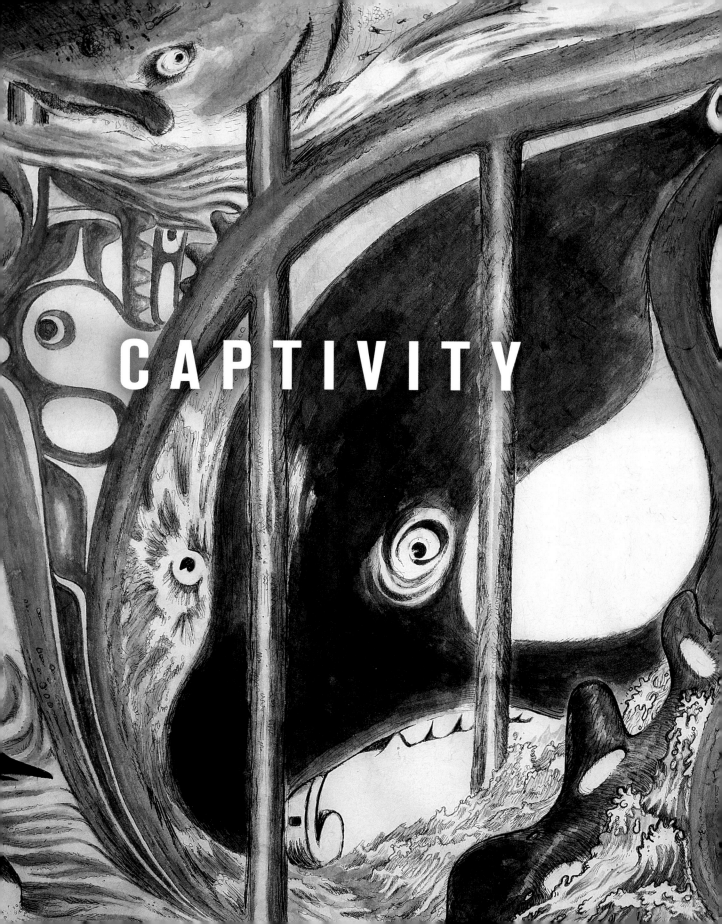

Killer Whale

bill bissett

'…I want to tell you love…'

Milton Acorn

we were tryin to get back to Vancouver
again cumming down th sunshine coast, away
speeding from th power intrigue of a
desolate town, Powell River, feudalizd
totally by MacMillian Blowdell, a diffrent
trip than when i was hitch-hiking back
once before with a cat who usd to live
next door to Ringo Starr's grandmother
who still lives in th same Liverpool house
in London, still shops at th same places
moves among th Liverpool streets
with th peopul, like she dusint want
to know, this cat told me

away from th robot stink there,
after th preliminary hearing, martina
and me and th hot sun, arguing
our way thru raspberry bushes
onto a bus headin for Van, on th ferry
analyzing th hearing and th bust, how
the whole insane trip cuts at our life
giving us suspicions and knowledge

K16 with chinook, 2014.
Ken Balcomb photo.

stead of innocence and th bus takes
off without us from th bloody B.C.
government ferry –I can't walk too good
with a hole in my ankle and all why
we didn't stay with our friends back
at th farm – destind for mor places
changes to go thru can feel th pull
of that heavy in our hearts and in th air,
the govrnment workmen can't drive us
20 minutes to catch up with th bus, insane
complications, phoning Loffmark works minister
in Victoria capital if he sz so they will they say
he once wrote a fan letter to me on an
anti-Vietnam pome publishd in Prism,"…with
interest…" he sd he read it, can't get him
on th phone, workmen say yer lucky if th
phone works, o lets dissolv all these phone
booths dotting surrealy our incognito intrigue
North American vast space, only cutting us all
off from each other – more crap with th bus
company, 2 hrs later nother ferry, hitch
ride groovy salesman of plastic bags, may
be weul work together we all laughing say

in th speeding convertibel to Garden City, he
wants to see there the captive killer whales.

down past th town along th fishing boat dock
th killer whales, like Haida argolite carvings,
th sheen- black glistening, perfect white circuls
on th sides of them, th mother won't feed
th baby, protests her captivity, why did they
cum into this treacherous harbour, th times
without any challenge, for food, no food
out there old timer tells me, and caught,
millions of bait surrounding them, part of
th systems, rather be food for th despondent
killer whales than be eat by th fattend ducks
on th shore there old timer tells me, and
if th baby dies no fault of mine th man
hosing him down strappd in a canvas sack
so he won't sink to th bottom, ive been hosing
him down 24 hrs a day since we netted em,
and out further a ways more killer whales
came in to see what was happening and they
got capturd for their concern, th cow howling,
thrashing herself in and out of the water, how
like i felt after getting busted, like we all
felt, yeah, th hosing down man told me, we got
enuff killer whales for 2 maybe 3 museums, course
th baby may die but there's still plenty for those
peopul whos nevr see animals like these
here lessen they went to a museum.

we went back to th convertible along th narrow
plank, heard the cow howl sum more, the bull
submerged, th man hosing th listless baby,
the sun's shattering light, them mammals aren't
going to take it lying down we thot, missd another
ferry connection, changd, made it staggerd
together into town. ⌇⟩⟩

Killer Whales I've Known
My Passage from Misunderstanding to Devotion

Steve Huxter

ORCAS TRAVELLED THE WATERS fronting the paper-mill town where I grew up on the mainland coast of the Strait of Georgia at the northern edge of the Salish Sea. I only ever saw them infrequently and from a distance as big, black shapes, with a fin like a shark.

I was ambivalent about marine mammals. I knew they were out there, but the chances of encountering one were low, so I wasn't curious and didn't much care as long as they didn't try to eat me.

My dad wasn't much for boating or fishing, but occasionally he would join one of his work buddies to go fishing for the day, hoping to bring home salmon for dinner. On one of these rare fishing trips, I remember my dad coming back early and empty handed, saying: "Charlie and I had the lines down, and the damn blackfish came straight for us. We pulled up our lines and cranked out of there before they got to us."

They felt that once the orcas were around, fishing was done for the day, because the salmon were spooked out of feeding, including on the fishing lures they trolled. The primary reason for "cranking out of there" was concern for their safety. They saw orcas as huge, powerful animals, capable of leaping out of the water to great heights, putting anyone in a small boat at risk. I took my dad's lesson and viewed orcas with the same caution.

In 1981, I moved from my small coastal town to the city of Victoria, BC. Canada was in a deep recession, and jobs were scarce. After three months of searching for work, I was about to swallow my pride and move back home.

(*Previous spread*) INTERSTELLAR SEA LIONS **PAUL MORSTAD**

IT WAS MIRACLE WHO SOFTENED MY HEART TOWARDS ORCAS.

With Haida and Tilikum. Jim Ryan photo.

A friend steered me towards a tourist attraction that might be hiring for the summer tourist season. I had never heard of the aquarium and didn't know it existed. I counted myself lucky for the opportunity to land a job.

After my interview and being hired to work in the gift shop, I was given a tour of the facility. I was completely taken by surprise to discover it housed seals, sea lions and two killer whales!

The first time that I viewed the whale shows, I stood at the handrail just behind the trainers at poolside and watched as the larger of the orcas lifted its head up onto the stage and opened its mouth for some fish. I saw, for the first time, that massive row of teeth, and I resisted the urge to step back.

During my orientation, I learned that the larger, seven-metre, six-tonne male orca was named Haida, and the smaller of the two was a young female called Miracle. They lived in separate pools. Miracle had been rescued by the aquarium a few years earlier. Born in the wild, she had been separated from her mother and pod, had a gunshot wound and injuries from what was thought to be a boat propeller, and was struggling with a serious infection.

It was Miracle who softened my heart towards orcas.

I was encouraged to familiarize myself with the performances, one of which was a show featuring Miracle. I was amazed to watch the trainers interacting with Miracle, stroking her and tickling her tongue— which she seemed to enjoy, because as the trainer walked away, she would propel herself up onto the deck of the stage as much as she could, sticking her tongue out as far as it would reach!

For me, the most mystifying thing happened after the performance. Visitors would often linger after the show, and I watched a pair of children doing their best to catch Miracle's attention, waving their arms and calling her name. She moved closer to them and lifted her head. At this acknowledgement, the kids moved along the handrails, encouraging her to follow, which she did. Before long the three were engaged in a game of chase, where the kids would run around to the opposite side of the pool and Miracle would chase after them.

It struck me … they're playing together, kids and a killer whale!

Ten months later, Miracle passed away, and less than a year after that, the other orca, Haida, died as well. The aquarium shut down. The company that owned the aquarium decided to rebuild and expand. Three orcas, two females and a male, were purchased from a company in Iceland that captured orcas to sell to aquariums. The two females, Haida II and Nootka, arrived first. The male orca, Tilikum, arrived some months later.

When Haida II and Nootka arrived, I was the administrative assistant for the aquarium. When one of the trainers unexpectedly left, I was asked to temporarily fill the empty spot by simply preparing food and doing general clean-up of the animal's areas while they searched for a new trainer. After two weeks, I requested a transfer to the animal care and training department. It was the beginning of the most transformative experience in my life.

In November of 1984, the third whale destined for the aquarium, Tilikum, was shipped from his holding pool in Iceland and made the long journey to Victoria. I was the first "trainer" to greet Tilikum when he arrived. By the time he had been captured, kept in a holding pool for many months and then flown to Victoria from Iceland, Tilikum had more experience interacting with humans than I had with orcas.

He was covered, head to fluke, with a lanolin-based cream to protect his skin during the long time he was out of the water, and after being lowered into the small pool that separated him from the two females who were to be his pool mates, Tilikum hesitatingly explored his new confines.

As I watched Tilikum glide around the pool, I crouched down and encouraged him toward me, a bucket of herring in my hand. I tapped the water's surface with a fish, and as Tilikum came close, I tossed the fish in front of him. He scooped it into his mouth and came closer still.

He stopped in front of me and raised his head, opening his mouth for more. I was taken aback.

This creature had just been trapped, separated from his family and removed

Meeting Tilikum. Provided by Steve Huxter.

I WAS OUT OF MY DEPTH AND STRUGGLED UNDER A LOAD OF INFORMATION AND FACTS ABOUT ORCA BEHAVIOUR OF WHICH I WAS COMPLETELY IGNORANT.

from his natural world. He had been slathered with goo, hung in a sling, flown thousands of kilometres and transported to the aquarium on a flatbed truck, and then a crane had lifted him into the air and lowered him into a tiny pool of water with concerned people milling about, and yet … despite all this … he looked up at me and seemingly trusted.

I was expecting distrust and hesitancy.

It must have been an incredibly frightening and uncomfortable journey, obviously perpetrated by people, yet he willingly engaged with me. I couldn't have said the same if our positions were reversed.

Over the next year and a half I learned how to guide the whales through performances, participated in medical checkups and made certain they received all the vitamins and medications they needed to keep them healthy.

When the head of the animal care and training department resigned, I was offered his position, and within a few weeks I was sent to attend a conference of the International Marine Animal Trainers Association.

A kiss from Haida. Jim Ryan photo.

At the meet and greet on the first day, I approached a group of folks and asked: "So, what kind of animals do you have at your aquarium?" and got the response: "Uhhh, actually we're doing micro-computer assisted training of dolphins for ergometric studies."

I was out of my depth and struggled under a load of information and facts about orca behaviour of which I was completely ignorant. During my first week back at the aquarium, I stood at poolside watching the three orcas under my care. The shift in my understanding was so dramatic I did the same thing for weeks afterward; just walking around their pool, watching every movement and interaction between them.

Previously, I had been careful not to attribute human behaviour characteristics to Haida, Nootka and Tilikum. Now, as the weeks and months passed and my insight grew, I could not help but see behaviour that I couldn't describe in any other way.

To watch as two of the orcas slowly glide in a synchronized swim around the pool, and in the moment, one delicately rubs a pectoral flipper against the other orca… a display of affection.

To see Haida take a piece of seaweed away from Nootka, and then to watch as Nootka bobs her head vigorously and darts away with a powerful sweep of her tail fluke… frustration.

They had a sense of fun, bordering on mischievousness. They had been taught, as part of the performances, to squirt a mouthful of water at the audience, which always elicited squeals and much arm waving as people scrambled to avoid a soaking. Apparently Haida, Nootka and Tilikum enjoyed the response, because on occasion they would do it on their own, enjoying the reaction of the visitors.

The pool they were in was a floating structure, and the walls were made of steel netting, which allowed seaweed to grow and would also allow small sea life to get into the pool. Looking to have a little fun, Nootka had squirted a mouthful of water towards some visitors, and along with the many litres of seawater was a big piece of seaweed she had plucked from the netting. One of the visiting youngsters threw the seaweed back into the pool for her, and Nootka promptly scooped it up and squirted it back up onto the deck.

And the game was on! After a couple times of the seaweed going back and forth, the youngster, now joined by a few other kids, ran to the opposite side of the pool and threw the seaweed in for Nootka, hoping she would follow them and continue the fun, which she did.

The kids were locals who would visit fairly regularly and play their game with Nootka. The day came when the kids visited and Nootka took control of the game. As usual, she gathered a piece of seaweed and would squirt it up to them, and the youngsters would throw it back to her. However, Nootka became the leader of the game and would quickly swim to the opposite side of the pool with the seaweed and squirt it up onto the deck, making the kids chase her around the pool to collect the prize! She had them breathless trying to keep up with her. Nootka had those youngsters very well trained!

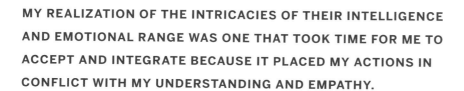

MY REALIZATION OF THE INTRICACIES OF THEIR INTELLIGENCE AND EMOTIONAL RANGE WAS ONE THAT TOOK TIME FOR ME TO ACCEPT AND INTEGRATE BECAUSE IT PLACED MY ACTIONS IN CONFLICT WITH MY UNDERSTANDING AND EMPATHY.

I remember a day when Nootka captured a small fish called a prickleback, which resembles a small eel. She squirted her toy at the kids as enticement to play the game, but it didn't go well. The squeamish youngsters were less than willing to pick up a live, squirming fish.

Along with all the variety of sea life that would make its way into their pool, at a certain time of the year, large schools of young herring would make their way into the pool. The first couple of years that Haida, Nootka and Tilikum experienced this bounty of food, they worked independently to catch the little fish. They darted about the pool using powerful sweeps of their tail flukes to lunge forward and make sharp turns and manoeuvres to catch their prey.

One year when the herring had returned, I was watching their hunting and noticed a change in technique.

In a seemingly coordinated effort, they approached the school of herring from three sides and slowly swam towards the fish, patiently guiding them towards a corner of the pool where they were contained in one tight mass of fish. Then, as if on cue, all three made a quick lunge forward with open mouths and clamped down on a mouthful of small herring.

I was truly astounded, and it was further testament to their intelligence. While it's true that other species have learned to hunt cooperatively using methods that have been developed over decades or centuries, these three orcas developed this cooperative hunting technique after only two previous occasions of the herring being in their pool, and on each occasion, the herring were only in the pool for two or three weeks before moving on.

I came to realize that these were not mere biological automatons, doing as we asked in return for a salmon or herring. They held cognitive ability and were creative thinkers!

With the passing of time, all these observations about their behaviour accumulated in my mind, and a shift in my understanding slowly took root.

My realization of the intricacies of their intelligence and emotional range

Tickling Haida's tongue. Provided by Steve Huxter.

was one that took time for me to accept and integrate, because it placed my actions in conflict with my understanding and empathy. I enjoyed the status of being a "killer whale trainer," and I'm embarrassed to admit that it fed my ego.

In the late 1980s, public pressure against keeping orcas in captivity increased. Then, in February 1991, the tragic drowning of a trainer who fell into the whale pool proved to be too much for the owner, and it was decided to close down the facility permanently. Haida, Nootka, Tilikum, and Haida's calf, Kyuquot, who was born at the aquarium, were sold, separated and moved to SeaWorld facilities in the United States.

That was the end of my career as an orca trainer, and I distanced myself from the industry until 2011, when my part in the documentary film *Blackfish* ignited my advocacy for orcas in captivity and those that are free.

Over the span of years, through my daily interactions with these absolutely amazing animals, I gained an understanding of the depth and breadth of their intelligence and emotional capabilities.

I learned that whales and dolphins are complex communicators, are highly social with lifelong family bonds, are cognitive thinkers with long-term memory, and experience a wide range of emotions. They display compassion and altruistic behaviour, are self-aware, and have distinct and unique personalities.

I once defended the holding of orcas in captivity, citing the value of research, education and the importance of the public forming a connection to the animal through their personal encounter, to foster empathy for the orcas and the environment in which they live.

It hasn't been effective.

Over the past 40 years there has been a 50 per cent decline in populations of animal life in the world's oceans. Oxygen levels have dropped as levels of carbon dioxide and ocean acidification increase. Despite our greater understanding, the very existence of orcas in the wild is threatened by lack of food and contamination of the oceans.

Throughout the years that I spent in the company of orcas, my thinking evolved from misunderstanding and distrust to profound admiration, and I count myself very fortunate to have stumbled into an opportunity that forever altered how I viewed not just orcas, but all animals with which we share our world.

The responsibility for their survival is ours, and ours alone. ⟿

(*Facing page*) JOY OF COMING HOME **FANNY AÏSHAA**

Learning to Love the Sea Wolves

Jason M. Colby

THE STORY WOULD SHAPE POPULAR VIEWS of orcas for decades. In January 1911, Robert F. Scott's much-heralded expedition to the South Pole reached Antarctica's Ross Island. Shortly after, Scott glimpsed killer whales nearby and asked journalist Herbert Ponting to photograph them. As Ponting approached, however, the orcas began breaking up the ice nearby, in the process nearly spilling the reporter and two expedition dogs into the sea. Perhaps they were just investigating; perhaps they mistook the dogs for Weddell seals—a common prey item. Whatever the reasons behind the behavior, Ponting had little doubt of the orcas' intentions, asserting that they had "turned about with the deliberate intention of attacking me." Although Scott wouldn't survive the ensuing trek to the South Pole, the tale of Ponting's near-death by "killers" did, receiving sensationalist coverage when Scott's journals were published in 1913. It was the first image many readers far from the sea had ever formed of the ominous predator often called the "sea wolf."

That reputation had been building for centuries. To be sure, there were examples of coexistence and even collaboration in some parts of the world. In Kamchatka, on the Sea of Okhotsk, Indigenous people sometimes hunted baleen whales in cooperation with orcas, and whalers in Eden, Australia, formed a similar relationship with killer whales in the 1830s. In the Pacific Northwest, Indigenous relations with the apex predator varied. Makah and nuučaanuɫ sometimes hunted orcas for food[1], while the Coast Salish focused primarily on salmon and largely coexisted with killer whales. In most of the world, however, the maritime industries framed a more adversarial view of *Orcinus orca*, whose Latin name could be loosely interpreted as "demon from hell." In Europe and later North America, commercial whalers, sealers and fishers referred to the species interchangeably as "orca" as well as

Ernest Linzell, *Attacked by Killer Whales*, ca. 1920.
Reproduced from Herbert G. Ponting, *The Great White
South* (London: Duckworth and Co., 1921).

"killer"—both terms conjuring a predator that competed for resources and potentially ate people. Writing in the 1870s, whaling captain Charles Scammon denounced orcas as "marine beasts" who spread "terror and death" to every ocean. Decades later, William Hornaday, the director of the Bronx Zoo, declared, "The killer whale, or orca, is the demon of the seas." Such depictions powerfully shaped news accounts of the species, particularly when it appeared to threaten valued marine resources. In April 1937, for example, the *New York Times* ran a story under the headline "Sea Wolves Kill Seals." Reporting that a group of killers were "ravaging" the seal rookeries of the Farallon Islands, just 20 miles west of San Francisco, the paper cast orcas as the "terror of the deep." The predators ate "seals of various kinds and especially the valuable fur seals of Alaska," the newspaper noted, asserting that "their annual toll on American industry amounts of several million dollars." And as in the case of wolves and other terrestrial predators, government policy sometimes aimed to eliminate killer whales. In Alaska, US officials regularly shot orcas passing the Pribilof Islands, where northern fur seals gathered to pup, and in the 1950s, NATO soldiers machine-gunned hundreds of orcas in the North Atlantic at the request of Icelandic herring fishermen.

It was a quirk of geography that made the Pacific Northwest the crucible of change. The region's population centres sat on Puget Sound, the Strait of Juan de Fuca, and the Strait of Georgia—a cross-border marine ecosystem now called the Salish Sea. This was also part of the main range of what scientists would later label the "Southern Resident killer whales," three pods (J, K, L) that rely primarily on chinook salmon. As late as 1880, they may have numbered 250, but commercial fishing and dams sharply reduced the chinook runs of the Sacramento and Columbia rivers. These changes likely drove the declining numbers of Southern Residents to spend more time foraging in the Salish Sea, where they competed with gigantic corporate-owned fish traps and a growing fleet of commercial fishing boats. For their part, fishers regarded them as threats to salmon harvests and regularly shot them on sight. In the first half of the twentieth century, newspapers on both sides of the border ran celebratory stories of locals killing orcas as well as seals and sea lions. Like pinnipeds, killer whales were considered vermin.

The scientists in the Pacific Northwest shared such views. Researchers at the US government's Marine Mammal Biological Laboratory in Seattle suspected the species harmed the whaling and sealing industries they managed, and they particularly worried that orcas were preying on northern fur seals, whose pelts were a valuable source of revenue for the US treasury. As a result,

IN 1960, PROMPTED BY COMPLAINTS FROM TOURISTS AND FISHING LODGES IN CAMPBELL RIVER THAT KILLER WHALES WERE DEPLETING CHINOOK SALMON, THE DEPARTMENT OF FISHERIES INITIATED ITS BLACKFISH CONTROL PROGRAM. AFTER CONSIDERING THE USE OF HARPOONS, MORTARS AND BOMBS TO KILL ORCAS, OFFICIALS FINALLY OPTED FOR A .50 CALIBER MACHINE GUN MOUNTED AT THE APPROACHES OF SEYMOUR NARROWS.

beginning in 1960, the lab instructed its researchers to harpoon killer whales and examine their stomach contents whenever the opportunity arose—a policy that resulted in the deaths of at least 10 orcas by 1967. At the time, such methods were standard practice among marine mammal scientists, most of whom followed the kill-and-dissect model of research. Like local fishers, scientists in the region thought little of shooting orcas and other marine mammals to further their goals.

Yet there was someone who offered a different perspective. G. Clifford Carl, director of the Royal BC Museum, had become interested in the species in the summer of 1945, when a pod of 20 orcas mysteriously stranded on the west coast of Vancouver Island near Estevan Point. When a local Indigenous man named Noah Paul first discovered them, several of the animals were still alive, with one young female having given premature birth, perhaps in an effort to free herself from shore. Carl learned of the whales weeks later and

came to examine their decaying bodies. He made careful measurements and sketches, as well as collecting a complete skeleton for the museum. He was hooked. Over the following years, he gathered all the information he could about killer whales in local waters, and he became especially obsessed with a unique white orca that frequented the waters around Vancouver Island. Dubbing the animal "Alice," Carl asked light keepers and Fisheries officials to report sightings of her, and his interest proved contagious. Soon the Victoria *Times* and Victoria *Colonist* were regularly reporting Alice's whereabouts, and by the 1950s locals made efforts to watch her from shore. Yet despite Carl's investigations, most northwesterners continued to regard orcas as dangerous pests.

Such thinking nearly led to catastrophe. In 1960, prompted by complaints from tourists and fishing lodges in Campbell River that killer whales were depleting chinook salmon, the Department of Fisheries initiated its Blackfish Control Program.

Spectators watch Alice, the white killer whale, near Victoria, BC, January 1958. Tim Sinclair photo. RBCM.

After considering the use of harpoons, mortars and bombs to kill orcas, officials finally opted for a .50 caliber machine gun mounted at the approaches of Seymour Narrows. Having recently eliminated basking sharks and much of the seal and sea lion populations to protect local fisheries, the Canadian government was now poised to remove the West Coast's apex predator. Thankfully, the gun was never fired at local orcas, and in those same years, at the height of human violence toward the species, live capture sparked a stunning change.

It all began by accident. In the summer of 1964, the Vancouver Aquarium harpooned a young killer whale, whose body it planned to use as a model for a sculpture in its new foyer. When the orca didn't die, staffers led it by harpoon line to Vancouver. Dubbed "Moby Doll," the youngster lived less than three months in captivity and was displayed publicly for only one day, but his docility surprised everyone. Like Alice, the animal spurred some observers to think of orcas as individuals for the first time. The following year, another accidental capture proved even more significant. In the summer of 1965, two fishermen near Namu, BC, accidentally trapped a large male orca behind their nets. Soon after, they sold the whale to Ted Griffin, the owner of the Seattle Marine Aquarium, who had long harboured dreams of befriending a killer whale. With the help of Indigenous workers, Griffin fashioned a floating pen and towed his new prize—named Namu—hundreds of kilometres south to Puget Sound. The voyage garnered news coverage around the world, and Griffin captured more headlines weeks later, when he slipped into the pen with Namu—the first known instance of a human swimming with an orca. To the surprise of reporters and scientists alike, Namu allowed Griffin to touch, scratch and eventually ride him. Soon thousands were visiting the Seattle waterfront each day to see the world's first choreographed orca shows. Featured in publications such as *National Geographic* and a Hollywood film entitled *Namu* (see pages 108–109), Griffin's bond with the orca had a twofold impact: first, the public marvelled at his gentleness with the aquarium owner and others who swam with the once-feared predator; second, Namu's popularity convinced oceanariums around the world to acquire their own killer whales, which quickly surpassed bottlenose dolphins as the marquee attraction. In the following years, Griffin supplied most of these captive orcas, including SeaWorld's

first "Shamu"—a young female whose name derived from "She-Namu." Orcas drew crowds, giving most visitors their first close-up view of orcas—and first sense of them as individuals. By 1970, some 30 million people had seen captive killer whales.

And the visitors weren't just spectators. Many were scientists with their first access to live orcas. It was in captive facilities that they first studied physiology, diving mechanisms and acoustic capacity, and it was also in such facilities that researchers came to know killer whales as individuals with their own unique personalities. The most influential of those individuals was Skana. Caught in Puget Sound and bought by the Vancouver Aquarium in March 1967, Skana didn't just draw visitors, she captivated a young researcher from New Zealand who was finishing his doctorate at UCLA. Hired to assess Skana's visual acuity, Paul Spong (see pages 133–140) designed a simple experiment that required the young orca to distinguish between two panels: one with a single line on it, and one with two. After answering correctly for weeks, Skana grew agitated one day and began answering the drills consistently and completely wrong. Frustrated and confused, Spong struggled to understand Skana's behavior. One day, as he dangled his feet in her pool and contemplated the nature of *Orcinus orca*, Skana surprised him by raking her teeth over his feet multiple

IN AUGUST 1970, GRIFFIN'S COMPANY UNKNOWINGLY CAPTURED ALL THREE PODS OF SOUTHERN RESIDENT KILLER WHALES IN PENN COVE OFF WHIDBEY ISLAND.

times, apparently studying his changing reaction. At first frightened, Spong soon realized that the tables had been turned: he had become the subject of Skana's own experiment. The impact on his thinking was profound. Convinced of Skana's sentience and troubled by the moral implications of her captivity, Spong left the aquarium to become a pioneer in wild orca research, as well as a leading critic of the industrial whaling that was decimating whale populations on the high seas.

Meanwhile, the live capture of orcas in the Salish Sea continued apace. In the late 1960s, fishermen on the Sunshine Coast sold more than a dozen killer whales to marine parks, including a female named Corky II, still on display at SeaWorld today. In March 1970, Bob Wright, owner of a small oceanarium near Victoria called Sealand of the Pacific, trapped a group of mammal-eating Transient killer whales, including a young female with striking white skin, almost certainly related to Alice. The capture received widespread public attention, as well as the endorsement of Chief Ed Underwood of the Tsawout First

Nation. Noting that the white orca was now Bob Wright's "whale spirit," Underwood predicted that "good fortune will not only knock once, but again and again at his door," provided Wright cared for the treasured animal.

Five months later, a massive capture south of the border focused unprecedented attention on Northwest orcas. In August 1970, Griffin's company unknowingly captured all three pods of Southern Resident killer whales in Penn Cove off Whidbey Island. Although Griffin immediately released half the animals, enraged activists tried to cut the rest free. The resulting collapse of the nets caused four young calves to drown. Griffin kept several other youngsters for sale, including Lolita—a young female who remains at the Miami Seaquarium 50 years later. Public backlash against the capture led to regulation of capture in Washington State and contributed to passage by the US Congress of the Marine Mammal Protection Act—the most sweeping legislation on treatment of marine mammals in history.

Although protection came more slowly in Canada, a "Save the Whales" movement was emerging in British Columbia, and it had close ties to orca captivity. After meeting writer Farley Mowat in Vancouver, Paul Spong lobbied Greenpeace—a new anti-nuclear activist group—to turn its attention to commercial whaling. In the process, he invited the organization's leader, Bob Hunter, to visit Skana at the Vancouver Aquarium. As cameras clicked, Skana nuzzled Spong and then surprised Hunter by taking his head gently in her mouth and holding it for several seconds. The moment proved transformative for Hunter, who joined Spong's crusade to stop commercial whaling. In the spring of 1975, the organization captured headlines when it confronted Soviet whalers off the California coast.

Meanwhile, captive orcas were facilitating a scientific revolution. In the early 1970s, Canadian researcher Michael Bigg, based at the Pacific Biological Station in Nanaimo, conducted the first population counts of wild killer whales in Northwest waters. He then turned to the challenge of understanding the species' migration patterns and social dynamics, which required a system of identifying and tracking individual animals. Working closely with orcas at Sealand—particularly a large male named Haida—Bigg designed a radio pack that

he attached to a wild male caught and released near Victoria in 1973.

Bigg also used this access to captive animals to develop a system for identifying individual orcas by their natural markings—particularly the shapes and marks on their dorsal fins and the patterns of their distinctive "saddle" patches. When he presented his findings, other scientists were resistant, with most arguing that the only way to identify individual orcas was to catch and mark them. Researchers had already experimented with the use of dry ice and even lasers to brand captured killer whales. Yet it was Bigg's non-invasive system that won out. In time, it made possible not only the identification of individual whales and the naming and tracking of distinct "pods," but also the realization that matrilineal connections shaped the organization and cultures of orcas in the Northwest and around the world.

That change in scientific and public perceptions in turn fueled rising opposition to capture. In 1975, when Sealand conducted another capture near Victoria, both Greenpeace and the BC government attempted to intervene. And when a young male sold to Marineland of Ontario was driven to the Victoria airport, protestors followed, demanding the whale be returned to his family. The following year, similar events took place in Puget Sound, when a SeaWorld team trapped several

Michael Bigg tries out a radio pack on Haida at Sealand of the Pacific, November 1973.
John F. Colby photo.

orcas in Budd Inlet, near the Washington State capital of Olympia. Protesters immediately surrounded the nets, and the Washington State government sued SeaWorld and the US government, effectively ending captures in Washington State. So profoundly had views of the species shifted by this time that when Paramount Pictures attempted to replicate the blockbuster success of Universal Studios' *Jaws* (1975) with *Orca: The Killer Whale* (1977), the film's plot of a violent and vengeful orca seemed absurd to most northwesterners.

That same summer, the people of the region were focused on a very different drama. In August 1977, a sports fisherman named Bill Davis happened upon a lone orca calf in Menzies Bay, just north of Campbell River. Lonely and hungry, she ate herring from his hand. Worried about the animal's health, Davis contacted Mike Bigg, who worked with Sealand to rescue the young orca. Moving her to the saltwater swimming pool at the Oak Bay Beach Hotel, Sealand staffers and local veterinarian Alan Hoey worked feverously to save the youngster, who had propeller and rifle wounds, likely inflicted by local fishermen. The whale sank to the bottom of the pool multiple times, her heart stopping on at least one occasion, but somehow she pulled through. The press dubbed her "Miracle," and over the following months some 3,000 came to see her each day. Among them were local children who worried the whale might die if she were released. As one teenaged boy wrote, "I love Miracle dearly, and I would like to see her grow up in Sealand and safe in Victoria!"

By early 1978, Miracle had nearly doubled in weight, and with winter storms threatening her pool, Sealand airlifted the orca to its main facility. There local reporters and researchers such as Alexandra Morton enjoyed the unique opportunity to interact with the whale in a captive setting. Miracle resided at Sealand at the Oak Bay Marina for the next four years, until she entangled and drowned in her net in January 1982. By that time, the live display and study of orcas had transformed perceptions of the species. "The most important result of the captive-orca era has been the almost overnight change in public opinion," observed writer-activist Erich Hoyt. "People today no longer fear and hate the species; they have fallen in love with them."

That love only grew in the following decades. By the early 1990s, whale-watching companies had appeared on both sides of the border, and officials who had once targeted orcas were now charged with protecting them. Among them was Victor Scheffer, a former researcher at the Seattle-based Marine Mammal Biological Laboratory. For decades, he had helped managed the northern fur seal harvest, and he had long considered orcas, like other marine mammals, primarily as specimens to be dissected. Yet he, too, had experienced the shifting environmental politics that carried an imperative to protect rather than exploit Pacific Northwest killer whales. Asked by a reporter in 1994 how he understood this change, Scheffer offered a simple response: "Seeing them in aquariums individualized these creatures, you see. They were no longer just whales in the abstract."

When Scheffer was interviewed, the Southern Resident orcas seemed to be enjoying a recovery, nearing 100 individuals by the late 1990s. That trend hasn't continued. In the past two decades, as the human population of the Salish Sea has spiked, the Southern Residents have dwindled. Today they number just 73, and although we enjoy them on both sides of the border, they rely primarily on the chinook runs of the Fraser River, near Vancouver, BC. Yet even as those chinook numbers continue to fall, the Canadian government has remained determined to push through expansion of the Trans Mountain Pipeline, not only threatening the Fraser River watershed but raising the danger of an oil spill similar

Angus Matthews, trainer of Sealand of the Pacific, "walks" Miracle, August 1977. Jim Ryan photo. Courtesy of Angus Matthews.

to that which devastated Alaska's Prince William Sound in 1989.

In light of the overwhelming threats facing the Southern Residents, some scientists and officials have asked whether attempting to save them is worth it. Aren't they simply victims of an evolutionary bottleneck doomed to extinction? Shouldn't we just let nature take its course? Yet such rhetoric ignores the degree to which we have damaged and denatured the ecosystem on which they rely. In that sense, the people of Canada and the United States might ponder a more compelling question. Considering what the Southern Resident orcas have given us and what we have taken from them, do we have a moral obligation to do everything possible to save them?

Clearly, we do. ➴

Notes

1 Charles M. Scammon, *Marine Mammals of the Northwestern Coast of North America* (San Francisco: J.H. Carmany, 1874), 92; Eugene Arima and Alan Hoover, *The Whaling People* (Victoria: Royal BC Musem, 2011), 59; and G. Clifford Carl, *A School of Killer Whales Stranded at Estevan Point, Vancouver Island* (Victoria: British Columbia Provincial Museum, 1945), B27.

Swimming into Popular Culture

Lorne Hammond

IN MAY 1964 orcas began to enter our popular culture. The failed killing of Moby Doll and subsequent attempt at veterinary treatment in a pen on the Fraser River began to stir public interest. Television, radio and newspapers offered glimpses of a new understanding of what fishermen called the killer whale, that apex predator. Reporters crouched on the dock interviewing scientists, and experts began to present the little that science knew about this unfamiliar sea monster. The curious drove down to take a look. The SPCA asked about ethics and began to square off against the director of the Vancouver Aquarium, who spoke of the educational value. Reporters asked, how do you feed them? Are they dangerous or gentle? How do you treat their injuries? It was all in all a very small, localized moment. In response to a reporter's question of value, a dollar figure of $20,000 US was invented on the spot as the value of a live orca.

That number reached two local fishermen up coast at the tiny BC coastal village of Namu. As they looked at fuel bills and an empty hold, they responded to storm warnings by spreading out nets to protect against entanglement during the storm. The next day they woke to find they had an accidental catch of two live orcas. They began making calls to aquariums, hoping to cash in. When one orca escaped, they worriedly dropped their price and settled for $8,000.

Reporters and a cameraman flew in on a floatplane to follow the towed pen being brought to an aquarium in Tacoma. The money to buy the orca had been loaned to Ted Griffin, the buyer, from local businesses at Tacoma's Pier 59. Anxious to promote the business, a full-on media communications campaign was launched.

Namu's hit record. Camelot J-120.
RBCM R2797.

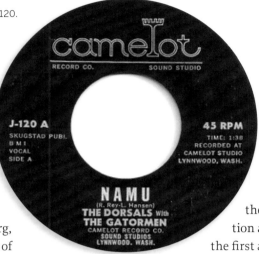

When Namu arrived on July 28, 1965, the public swarmed to the dock, as did the media, on what Tacoma's mayor declared "Ted Griffin and Namu Day." Even John Cherberg, the lieutenant governor of Washington State, attended. Media pronounced the orca an economic engine for waterfront redevelopment and a cornerstone for tourism. Griffin, deeply in debt, copyrighted Namu's name and set up Namu Inc. to produce T-shirts and souvenirs. At what became the Seattle Marine Aquarium, more than 100,000 would buy tickets to see the orca over the next five weeks.[1]

As part of the welcome, Tacoma recording engineer Jan Skugstrad had already assembled a rock 'n' roll studio band named the Dorsals (with the Gatormen) and quickly produced a seven-inch 45 rpm record, "Namu," combining human vocals with Namu's vocalizations and with an instrumental called "Killer Whale" on the B-side.[2]

With it came the quickly designed killer whale dance, performed at Pier 59 by two young women in fringed bikinis, with the Dorsals performing live behind them. Local papers printed out the killer whale dance steps, and Namu was the first orca to have a hit record on local radio stations.

And so it began: the capture, transportation and sale of live orcas; the first aquarium display; the appearance of orcas in pop culture; and the public's fascination with them. From killers to be shot they were becoming an economic commodity, one that could be sold, trained and traded. Aquariums in Vancouver, Victoria, Florida and California all assessed the media focus, the level of public interest and the profitable attendance numbers and wondered how they could acquire their own live orcas.

Ted Griffin set out to capture a mate for Namu, but in the capture a mother was harpooned, and she sank and drowned only metres from her calf. The calf refused to respond to aquarium staff or Namu and was sold to California's SeaWorld. Initially they wanted to license the name Namu to cash in on the success of Tacoma. Griffin refused, and the young calf was renamed Shamu. It was with Shamu that the full

Souvenir pennant, late 1970s.
RBCM R2806.

process of commodification occurred. A carefully rehearsed full performance before theatre-seated visitors, the splash spectacular Shamu Show was a hit replicated at other SeaWorld aquariums in Florida and around the world. Other orcas were taught to do the Shamu Show. Shamu became the first orca corporate brand.

Namu also caught the attention of Hollywood. In the mid-1960s nature films had a ready market. There was John Wayne's *Hatari!* (1962), a film about live capture on the African savannah, and the television spin-off *Daktari* (1966–1969), about a veterinarian and his daughter saving animals from poachers. It featured another ferocious predator, Clarence, a cross-eyed lion, and his court-jester friend, a chimpanzee. In the aquarium, seals and dolphins were the court-jesters, trained to perform amusing tricks before the "tamed" star orca came on. There was also the popular aquatic television show *Flipper* (1964–1967), about two young boys and their intelligent dolphin friend. The timing was perfect for something bigger—was it orcas? So United Artists hoped when they arrived in Tacoma. As Jason Colby pointed out in his book *Orca*, one of the most dramatic moments in the interaction of humans and orcas happened in Tacoma, when a filmmaker asked if it was safe to get in the water with Namu. Ted Griffin became the first human to enter a tank and swim with a killer whale.[3] The deal was set.

Namu had died on July 6, 1966, after a year in captivity, before the August release of *Namu, the Killer Whale* (later re-released as *Namu, My Best Friend*). Director László Benedek (1905–1992), a Hungarian émigré who fled the Nazis, had also directed *Death of a*

Shamu merchandise. RBCM R2821, R2819, R2823.

Tom Glazer Sings the Ballad of Namu the Killer Whale.
United Artists Records UAL 3540, 1966. RBCM R2891.

Salesman (1951) and Marlon Brando's debut, *The Wild One* (1953). Blacklisted during the Red Scare, he turned to television. His cast from *Namu* would go on to shows like *General Hospital* and *Barnaby Jones*.[4] His underwater cameramen had already worked with sharks. The film was perfect for contemporary 1960s family entertainment. Its star was a little girl who would make the connection between humans and orcas, and its marketing slogan, "Make Room in Your Heart for a Six-Ton Pet!"

The plot weaves several themes common to Hollywood films about orcas. Science is represented by Hank Donner, an ethical marine biologist curious about understanding the sounds a grieving orca makes. His love interest, Kate Rand, is a fisherman's widow who sells salmon nets. Despite local talk that her husband may have been killed by an orca, she decides to support Hank in protecting the orca.

Her daughter Lisa is the curious child who befriends the grieving orca whose mate was killed by fishermen. All are healed by the end of the story. Hank introduces an Indigenous theme, telling Lisa an Umatilla creation story about an island split off from the coast by an earthquake and a fearsome creature named Namu (meaning "whirlwind", according to the film) who gives a young Indigenous princess a ride on its back to the island of her people.

The local fishing community plots to shoot the orca before the impending seasonal return of the salmon back from the deep ocean. Lisa shares her bond with Namu with local children, but a teenage boy tries to feed Namu bait filled with fish hooks, causing screaming pandemonium. In a mob, the community arrives to protect their children, including mothers toting shotguns. The hooked bait is recovered, confessions occur, and Hank and Kate feed and swim with the orca to show his gentleness. But one last, determined holdout arrives by boat to shoot the orca. Hank orders the nets opened to free Namu from the bay. Namu overturns the bad man's boat and swims off without harming him (as happens in *Free Willy 3*), rejoining his pod and new mate, swimming out to sea and freedom, having taught humans that while powerful, they are not killers, and that family, ashore or at sea, means everything. Over the credits the folk musician Tom Glazer sings:

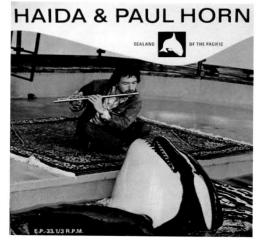

Haida and Paul Horn E.P. record. Sealand of the Pacific, 1972. RBCM R2798.

Live and let live,
Let nature be your teacher.
Respect the life of your fellow creature.
Live and let live, whatever you do
and always remember the
killer whale Namu.[5]

As a film *Namu* is a potent mix: Indigenous origin stories are recounted; a child of nature calms a ferocious beast; families are healed; interspecies communications are attempted by both human and orca; the economic conflict over salmon as a food source for both is addressed but not resolved. It is at heart a morality tale about artificial boundaries and perceptions that net a line between their world and ours.

Back in Victoria, at the Oak Bay Marina, local entrepreneur Bob Wright opened Sealand of the Pacific on May 17, 1969, complete with Junior the Orca in a one-million-gallon fresh-seawater net-walled tank. Local radio station CFAX ran a naming contest, and the female orca became known as Nootka. Two more orcas were added, a male called Haida and a young female albino named Chimo, captured off Race Rocks.

In 1972 the National Film Board of Canada commissioned a short documentary filmed at Sealand of the Pacific. *We Call Them Killers* records an early show and introduces orca researcher Paul Spong (see pages 133–140), who is seen working with orcas as he explains their unique sensory world. Jazz flautist Paul Horn makes an appearance improvising music with Haida, and a seven-inch 33 1/3 rpm record was subsequently released with narration about those first orca/human musical improvisations.

Paul Spong's call for the release of orcas after five years would go unheaded for several decades.[6]

Hollywood views of orcas had swung back to "killer" in 1975, in part because of another

Opening day, Marineland of the Pacific. Daily Colonist, May 17, 1969, p. 7.

109

Orca movie poster, 1977. RBCM R2813.

Facing page: The first Haida, Sealand of the Pacific, ca. 1973–1974. Jim Ryan photo.

cinematic predator: the great white shark in Steven Spielberg's *Jaws*, the highest-grossing film of all time before *Star Wars*. Box office profits drove Dino De Laurentiis to produce *Orca: The Killer Whale* (1977) about something bigger and more dangerous–something that preys on great whites. In Newfoundland, the fictional Captain Nolan (Richard Harris) sets out to capture a great white for an aquarium, but finds bigger game when an orca saves his scuba-diving scientist. Nolan harpoons and hauls onboard a pregnant female, who miscarries and dies. The mother and dead orca calf are thrown over the side in view of the enraged male orca.

Vengeance and mayhem ensue: the orca knocks the pilings out from under the captain's waterfront home, and it slides into the sea; Bo Derek makes her film debut (the orca bites off her leg); the town dock collapses; fish boats sink; broken fuel lines ignite. Charlotte Rampling plays a marine biologist who tries to resolve things, but after his crew dies one after another, Captain Nolan, like Melville's Ahab chasing Moby Dick, meets his fate harpoon in hand. Unlike Ahab, he is tail-slapped into an iceberg (made in Malta). The orca swims off under the ice, its grief and vengeance complete.

Aside from some interesting biological details on how Arctic orcas hunt, the old family-oriented 1960s message is replaced by gritty male human/orca 1970s vengeance violence. The lessons of Namu are undone. But even here, there is a space created for Indigenous perspectives, delivered by Native American actor William Sampson, Jr. (1933–1987), better known as "Chief" in *One Flew Over the Cuckoo's Nest* (1975). Interspecies male violence, the nuclear family motif, an Indigenous connection, grief and orca intelligence are all there.

Miracle spitting at the audience at Sealand of the Pacific, ca. 1979–1980. Jim Ryan photo.

This film overshadowed an odd, obscure low-budget film made off Alert Bay, British Columbia. *Jaws of Death* (1977) involves divers and kayakers trying to communicate with orcas using synthesizers, and includes orca expert Erich Hoyt as a scientist (much to his later embarrassment). Almost impossible to find, it sank with barely a trace, in part because of a similarly named shark-sploitation film *Mako: Jaws of Death* (1976). As one critic pointed out, the Alert Bay film also lacked a screaming girl on its poster and any women in the cast.[7]

A more dramatic real story followed in 1977, as a young orca, shot, starving and near death, was rescued by Nanaimo fisherman Bill Davis. Trucked down to Sealand and slowly nursed back to health, the whale was named Miracle and taught to perform. But Sealand was under increasing pressure from local activists, and the 1982 death of Miracle, drowned in a cut net, remains a mystery. Who made the anonymous call taking responsibility? Two documentaries were made about Miracle: a half-hour CHEK-TV television program about the rescue of the whale and Scott Renyard's 2009 documentary about Miracle's death.[8]

In 1993 the blockbuster return to a Namu worldview happened with Warner Bros.' *Free Willy*. Made with a budget of $20 million, it took in $150 million, captivating global audiences. It used a combination of shots of a young orca, an animatronic orca based on the technology developed for *Jaws*, and early CGI, particularly for the climactic leap-to-freedom sequence.

Returning to the Pacific Northwest, the film opens with a Penn Cove–like capture scene as Willy is taken from his family, with sounds of orca terror. Jesse, a troubled youth from a foster home, breaks into the aquarium theme park and discovers a captured orca behind a glass tank wall. Arrested for trespassing and graffiti, his sentence is to work under a kindly Haida tank keeper, Randolph, played by Mohawk actor August Schellenberg (1936–2013). Jesse forms a bond with the orca.[9] Randolph shares Indigenous knowledge with Jesse, including the Haida story of the storm boy who went below the waves to the home of the orcas. He is given a pendant and a powerful prayer by Randolph. He meets a young girl who dreams of being a marine biologist, and she and Randolph watch as Jesse and Willy develop an aquarium performance together.

Jesse finds himself when he foils a plan to drain the tank and kill Willy for insurance money. The trio, led by Jesse and now joined by his foster parents, take the whale to the ocean. In the climax, as boats full of evil men with rifles and nets close in, he recites a Haida prayer to give Willy the strength to perform a CGI leap over a stone breakwater to freedom. Jesse returns to bond with his adoptive parents.

The original *Free Willy* VHS includes extras: the Michael Jackson theme song, which won an MTV award; an advertisement for the Earth Institute for Marine Mammals, endorsed by Bumble Bee Tuna, which committed to being dolphin friendly.

More than a Hollywood orca film, *Free Willy* sent a global wave of ocean and orca stewardship values out to millions of children, families, teachers and classrooms.

Free Willy had several sequels, set between Vancouver Island and Haida Gwaii, which tackled illegal fisheries and orca capture and showed the birth of an orca

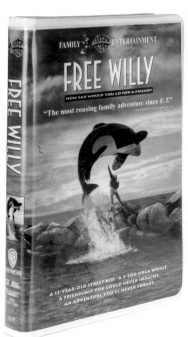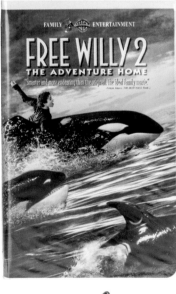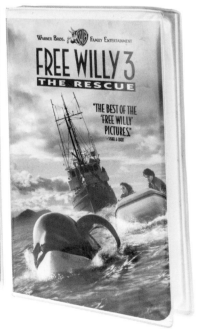

Free Willy 1–3 VHS tapes. Reproduction of Jesse's necklace, Free Willy Keiko Foundation. RBCM R2808.1–3; R2828.

KEIKO WAS THE FIRST AND THE MOST COMPLEX ATTEMPT AT REINTRODUCTION OF ORCAS INTO THE WILD, WITH DOZENS OF FAILED ATTEMPTS TO REINTRODUCE HIM TO DIFFERENT PODS.

Orca activist buttons, 2019. RBCM R2830.

calf. In the sequels, Jesse and Free Willy grew into adulthood together.[10]

There is a story within the story of *Free Willy* about Keiko, the real orca in the film. After the deaths of so many orcas in the infamous 1972 Penn Cove round-up, the capture of orcas was made illegal in Washington State. Live capture shifted to Iceland. A two-year-old orca was captured there in 1979 and sold to an aquarium in Hafnarfjörður, near the capital, Reykjavík. He was named Siggi and then Kago before being sold in 1982 to Canada's Marineland at Niagara Falls, where he was bullied by the two older, non-Icelandic orcas, and his health declined. Renamed Keiko (a Japanese woman's name meaning "blessed child"), he was sold again in 1985 to Latin America's biggest amusement park, Reino Aventura, in Mexico City. It was here the scouts for *Free Willy* found him. Little Keiko was the perfect size for close-up shots with Jesse, and a camera crew arrived. After the film, he grew to double

his length, enclosed in a small, shallow warm-water tank built for dolphins.

Craig and Wendy McCaw of Seattle read an article by Ken Balcomb about Keiko's desperate condition and decided to become involved. They established the Free Willy Keiko Foundation to free him.

Children around the world raised money, and Warners agreed to share its profits. In 1996, Keiko was transported to a massive new rehabilitation tank in Newport, Oregon. Two years later he was flown home to Iceland, but the giant transport plane's landing gear collapsed during the landing at Vestmannaeyjar airport. Rescued from the plane crash, Keiko was acclimatized in a pen in a nearby bay. He took day trips to learn to hunt and to meet other pods, but he always returned to his humans. In 2002, he left Iceland and swam to Norway. There he continued to rely on humans and avoid local orcas. Keiko was the first and the most complex attempt at reintroduction of orcas into the wild, with dozens of failed attempts to reintroduce him to different pods.[11] As sponsors fell away, the foundation maintained their support. Keiko swam free in Norway until his death by pneumonia in 2003. His release was the direct result of a film, a wealthy family, and fundraising from children.

The darkest film about orcas changed public attitudes to aquariums dramatically. *Blackfish* (2013) begins in Iceland, where a whale was captured in 1982 and sold to Sealand of the Pacific in Victoria, British Columbia. He was given a local name, Tilikum. He would be involved in the deaths of three humans. The first occurred in Victoria. Local 21-year-old environmental studies student and competitive swimmer Keltie Byrne worked part-time as a trainer. On February 20, 1991, Keltie slipped and fell into the whale tank at Sealand. The three orcas, Haida II, Nootka and Tilikum, submerged her and dragged her around the pool. Three times she tried to climb out and was dragged back by her foot. Battered and submerged, Keltie drowned. Staff tried in vain to rescue her, and it took several hours to recover her body. In February 1992 Tilikum was transferred to SeaWorld in Orlando, Florida. He was used in a breeding program and trained to perform in the Shamu Show.

Seven years later, Daniel Duke evaded SeaWorld security to stay overnight and swim naked with the whale. His body was found in the tank with the orca in the morning. The coroner found no trace of drugs or alcohol. There were no witnesses. Tilikum continued to perform until February 24, 2010, when, at the conclusion of the Dine with Shamu Show, he pulled his longtime trainer Dawn Brancheau into the water and killed her. Controversy over the initial statement that the death was accidental (an entangled ponytail) resulted in Gabriela Cowperthwaite's film connecting the other two deaths.

Subsequently over 40 incidents involving orcas and trainers led to a work safety ruling against the aquarium. Tilikum was retired from performing in 2011. As part of the aquarium breeding program, he sired 21 orcas in captivity. Today, two-thirds of aquarium orcas have never been in open oceans.

Released in 2013, *Blackfish*, which began as a film about one death and one orca, indicted the entire aquarium industry and argued that trauma from containment was a factor. The film and the workplace safety ruling became the turning point in the battle for public opinion between animal rights activists and aquariums, giving us a far darker vision than the fictionalized and overly simplified world of greed portrayed in *Free Willy*.

Which brings us to our most recent vision of an orca. It is one that combines mystery, lightness, community divisions, spiritual dimensions and, yes, grief. It took place in Gold River, British Columbia, a very small community dependent on fishing and fish farms, logging and tour-

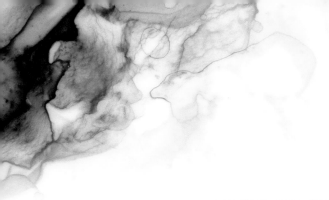

HUMANS HAVE THREE NAMES FOR HIM: SCIENTISTS CALLED HIM L98, THE MOWACHAHT/MUCHALAHT CALLED HIM TSU'XIIT, AND NON-INDIGENOUS ACTIVISTS AND MEDIA CALLED HIM LUNA.

ists. It is near where Captain Cook first met the Indigenous Mowachaht/Muchalaht community. It is also an occasional feeding ground for the Southern Resident L pod, visiting from US waters. All of these stakeholders and more would be drawn into the story of Luna.

Two days after the death of Chief Ambrose Maquinna, who had promised to return as a whale, a lone orca appeared. Humans have three names for him: scientists called him L98, the Mowachaht/Muchalaht called him Tsu'xiit, and non-Indigenous activists and media called him Luna. Over the next five years, Luna became a local celebrity and sparked an ecotourism boom. But his boat-racing and near collisions alarmed Fisheries and Oceans Canada officials. American orca organizations, fresh from the successful capture, rehabilitation and release of Springer in 2002, sought to have Luna captured and reunited with his pod. Public pressure mounted on both the Canadian and US governments. Earth Watch and the Free Willy Keiko Foundation drew up plans for a safe move. Vancouver Aquarium experts joined Fisheries and

Oceans Canada (DFO) discussions. Local orca activists, embedded in the community, were critical, while the Mowachaht/Muchalaht took offense at arbitrary DFO actions in their traditional territory and a lack of respect for their spiritual connections. Tensions built, but there was also humour. One attempt to herd Luna into a floating pen ended with Luna pushing the boat into the pen and swimming off.

Luna sparked an intensely complex and intricate discussion about human/orca interaction and dependency. On March 10, 2006, Luna was drawn into the blades of a powerful deep-sea industrial tug and killed. The captain of the tug, who knew the young orca, was devastated. The community went into shock.

The repercussions and the impact on the community of the arrival, life and death of one lone orca was portrayed in a fictionalized CTV television drama with Jason Priestley and Tantoo Cardinal. Suzanne Chisholm and Michael Parfit's award-winning documentary *Saving Luna* had not one but two releases. After the initial theatrical release and a CBC national broadcast, it was recut, narrated and produced by Vancouver's Ryan Reynolds and Scarlet Johansson and released as *The Whale* (2011). Unlike Springer, an orca reunited with her family, Luna, like Keiko, was alone, and sought human company. Or was he Chief Maquinna, moving between worlds? Luna reflects our current place in the rich complexity of stories we tell ourselves about orcas.

Throughout all these films, the threads of science, Indigenous knowledge or voice, interspecies communication and cooperation, violence, the actions of children, the nature of freedom and our yearning for connections seem a constant. Of all of these factors, science seems to receive far less importance than the emotional connection.

Yet we are not orcas. We do not see the world through orca's eyes, only our own. These are only films, images and sounds that record the stories we tell ourselves about orcas. As I write this, Canada's legislation ending captivity for orcas and dolphins (Bill S-203) has just passed final reading.[12]

These films have become our history. They reflect how our ideas have changed and evolved, and how we have responded to what orcas teach us about our world and theirs. ꩜

Notes

1   Jason M. Colby. *Orca: How We Came to Know and Love the Ocean's Greatest Predator* (Oxford: Oxford University Press, 2018), 81.

2   *Namu/Killer Whale,* Camelot Records Co. Catalog no. J-120. Recorded in 1965 at Camelot Studio, Lynnwood, Washington. *Namu* was Jan Kurtis Skugstad's biggest hit among his 40 local teen records. He also made recording history with the definitive live recording of his former bandmates, Ernest Tubb's Texas Troubadours, and recorded John Coltrane's live Seattle performance. "Camelot," *Recording Studios of the Pacific Northwest (1940s–1960s)* by Peter Blecha Posted July 26, 2009. historylink.org/File/8946

3   Colby, *Orca,* 87.

4   Born in Budapest in 1905, Benedek studied medicine in Berlin, paid for by making films, until he fled to Hollywood, where he became a protégé of Stanley Kramer. His now-classic films were financial flops. Friendship with Communists marginalized him in Hollywood, and he turned to television, directing *Rawhide* and *The Untouchables*. See William Honanmarch, "Laslo Benedek, 87, Film Director Known for 'Wild One,' Is Dead," *New York Times*, March 14, 1992. www.nytimes.com/1992/03/14/arts/laslo-benedek-87-film-director-known-for-wild-one-is-dead.html

5   Thomas Zachariah Glazer (1914–2003). Born of Russian immigrants from Minsk, the three Glazier brothers lost their father in 1918 to influenza in Philadelphia. Alan Lomax encouraged Tom to learn guitar at the Library of Congress Archive of American Folk Song. By the 1940s, he had a radio program where he sang songs on social issues. Blacklisted, he was a well-known songwriter, performing with Pete Seeger, Oscar Brand and the Weavers. In

1960 Bob Dylan recorded his "Talking Inflation Blues." He disliked his biggest hit from his 1963 children's show, "On Top of Spaghetti." "Obituary: Tom Glazer, Folk Singer, Is Dead at 88," *New York Times,* Feb 26, 2003. www.nytimes.com/2003/02/26/arts/tom-glazer-folk-singer-is-dead-at-88.html?pagewanted=1 http://20thcenturyhistorysongbook.com/song-book/post-world-war-ii/blacklisting

6   *We Call Them Killers*, National Film Board, 1972. The trainer in the NFB film, Mark Perry, is interviewed in Eric Burgoyne, "Conversation with Whales," *Times Colonist, The Islander,* December 5, 1972, 10–11. Underwater photographer Allan Hook recounts Nootka biting through his suit and skin and taking a chunk out of his flipper (though the trainer was more concerned about the orca swallowing the rubber), an ominous prequel to later events that ended in the death of a trainer. "Diving With Whales," *Time Colonist, The Islander,* March 18, 1973, 10–11.

7   *Jaws of Death* (1977). Directed by Richard Martin, whose father was in *Rowan & Martin's Laugh-In*. Its competition was *Mako: Jaws of Death* (1976) by William Grefé, about a loner whose amulet gives him telepathic abilities to talk with sharks. He kills shark exploiters and meets a mermaid in a bar, but he is himself eaten by sharks when he loses his medallion. Jesse also wears an Indigenous medallion in the *Free Willy* films.

8   *Miracle, the Killer Whale*, CHEK-TV, 1977. BC Archives AAAA2232. *Who Killed Miracle?* Dir. Scott Reynard. Juggernaut Productions and Horizon Motion Pictures, 2009.

9   August Schellenberg (July 25, 1936–August 15, 2013) was of Mohawk and Swiss-Canadian ancestry. He had a distinguished, award-winning career as an actor. He reprised his role as Randolph in the sequels to *Free Willy*. His remarkable career included many films about Indigenous history, both historical (*Black Robe*, 1991; *Tecumseh*, 1995; *Bury My Heart at Wounded Knee*, 2007) and contemporary (*Siege at Ruby Ridge*, 1996). His favourite role was that of Sitting Bull. He performed on stage with Tantoo Cardinal at Canada's National Theatre in the landmark all-Indigenous cast of *King Lear*

in 2012 and mentored many of the next generation of Indigenous actors in acting workshops. He died at his home in Dallas, Texas.

10   *Free Willy*, Warner Bros. (1993). The sequels included *Free Willy 2: The Adventure Home* (1995), set two years later, which involves saving Willy's pod (including a sibling called Luna) from a tanker oil spill. An evil oil executive claims to be rescuing the orcas for rehabilitation, but plans to sell them to a theme park. At the last minute the plot is revealed and the orcas led to freedom through a burning oil slick. In *Free Willy 3: The Rescue* (1997), a research ship turns out to be a front for an illegal whale hunt to kill orcas and sell them for exotic sushi. The plot is revealed, and the pirate whalers' plans are foiled. The most interesting aspect is the rescue of Willy's mate and the live birth of Willy's son. Less well known is *Free Willy 4: Escape From Pirate Cove* (no theatre release, 2010). Set in South Africa, it stars a young Australian teenager, Kirra (Bindi Irwin), and her grandfather (Beau Bridges). Horrified at a deal to sell Willy to a corporation, Kirra and Sifiso (Siyabulela Ramba) return Willy to freedom and his pod.

11   M. Simon, M.B. Hanson, L. Murrey, J. Tougaard and F. Ugarts. "From Captivity to the Wild and Back: An Attempt to Release Keiko the Killer Whale," *Marine Mammal Science*, July 2009, Volume 25, Issue 3, 693–705.

12   After three years of senate review and amendments, the Ending the Captivity of Whales and Dolphins Act (Bill S-203) passed the third and final reading in Canada's senate on June 10, 2019. On June 21, 2019 the bill became law. It amended the Criminal Code; added $200,000 fines; changed the Fisheries Act and the Wild Animal and Plant Protection and Regulation of International and Interprovincial Trade Act; and explicitly acknowledged pre-existing Indigenous rights. The bill provides for protection of mammals already present in facilities, protects aquarium staff from prosecution, permits legitimate research and emergency rehabilitation of animals in distress, and bans breeding and trade in reproductive materials. Over 60 per cent of all aquarium orcas were born in captivity.

Facing page: "Jump!" Haida, Sealand of the Pacific, ca. 1977. Jim Ryan photo.

IT'S COMPLICATED **MATT WHELAN**

J pod south of Clover Point, Victoria, BC, 2014.

Collecting Culture

Gavin Hanke

T ALL STARTED IN THE SALISH SEA: science on orca behaviour, population surveys, the study of orca vocalization, activism, and of course, the harvest. Southern Resident orcas were taken from the eastern North Pacific Ocean and scattered around the world to feed an insatiable aquarium industry. One was an orca named Cuddles, taken from Yukon Harbor, Puget Sound, and for a short time held at Flamingo Land in northern England. He was eventually moved to the Dudley Zoo in England in 1971, not seven kilometres from where I was born. Cuddles's family had been ripped apart. He travelled alone. By the time he died in 1974, my own pod had started the opposite journey, west towards the Salish Sea.

My next contact with an orca was in the summer of 1973 at Marineland in Niagara Falls, during the heyday of orca capture for aquarium exhibition. The whale I saw, Kandu 2, was from L pod, and like Cuddles came from the Salish Sea. Kandu 2 was captured in Washington at Penn Cove in 1971. A decade earlier, shooting orcas had been totally acceptable, even encouraged, and the Save the Whales movement had yet to be conceived.

As a child, I was amazed by the size of the "killer whale," but I didn't think anything about the size of its enclosure or its pointless performance. Like countless thousands, my first encounter with an orca was at a public aquarium. We marvelled at the sight of an orca blasting skyward to nudge a mooring ball. We didn't know about the horrors at Penn Cove. I was there the summer Kandu 2 was reunited with another L pod relative, imaginatively named Kandy. Kandy was caught in Pedder Bay, Vancouver Island, in 1973. She died that same year at Marineland. I continued west.

The movie industry provided my next thrilling orca encounter, with Bo Derek losing an appendage to an orca seeking vengeance for the death of its mate and child. Hot on the heels of *Jaws*, *Orca* was a monster movie,

An old family photo of Kandu 2, Marineland, Niagara Falls, 1973. June Parkinson photo.

or at least that was how I remembered it. Fast forward to December 1991, and orcas featured on my round-trip from Winnipeg to Victoria. By this time my pod was scattered, but for us it was by choice. An announcement came over the ferry loudspeakers: "For those who are interested, there's a pod of killer whales off the starboard bow."

My first ferry ride—my first trip to the Pacific coast of British Columbia, and wild orcas alongside! I was one of very few people who bothered to look, or who knew ship anatomy well enough to look in the right direction. I can still point to the exact spot in Active Pass decades later. That same trip included a visit to Sealand in Oak Bay, and another close look at an orca in an "aquarium." I don't know who tried to spray me with a mouthful of water, but this was my first and only one-on-one encounter with an orca. It could have been Haida II, Nootka IV or even Tilikum—I probably saw all three.

Years of university came to an end in 2001. My dad said, "You'll never get a job with that degree." Fortunately, he was wrong. I was hired right away as the curator of zoology for the Manitoba Museum, and then about a year and half later, the Royal BC Museum allowed me to focus a bit as their curator of vertebrate zoology. This time the trip from Winnipeg to Victoria was one way. Sealand was closed, its three orcas shipped away. By the time I settled in Victoria, Haida II and Nootka IV were dead. Tilikum was at SeaWorld in Orlando. I was free to sail and kayak in Southern Resident orca habitat.

I witnessed the media storm surrounding the presence of Luna (L98) in Nootka Sound, the children at Miracle Beach Elementary School singing on the morning radio, and Luna's death. I saw a pod of orcas while salmon fishing off Sooke, and many more during research trips along our coast and sailing excursions in the Salish Sea. Orcas were everywhere, even on beer bottle caps. I remember kayaking around the south end of Trial Island when a sizable pod swam by. I

Albino orca. BC Archives photo.

waited close to shore, but they likely knew I was there. While waiting, I counted 32 boats leap-frogging this pod, years before the 400-metre exclusion zone existed. This was when I first started to take notice of our impacts on our aquatic neighbours.

As a kayaker and sailor, I didn't think I had an impact on orcas, but as a sushi/ sashimi fanatic, I was eating a lot of raw salmon. I was a competitor drawing energy from the sea, and as far as salmon consumption was concerned, on the same trophic level as the local Southern Resident orcas. As a newly minted curator, I also was responsible for building a portion of the museum's collection for scientific research, including research on orcas. The kid from England was now an orca scavenger.

The Royal BC Museum's collection of orcas spans seven decades. Our first specimen came from Cherry Point, Vancouver Island, in the 1940s. Clifford Carl, a zoologist, was the museum's director, and he may have been the first to use citizen science to understand orca migration, by drawing public attention to a uniquely marked orca (an albino). Today a huge network of citizen scientists use unique markings to identify, census and track orcas following ground-breaking work by Dr. Michael Bigg.

The museum now has 23 orca specimens in its collection. We have animals representing BC's Southern Residents, Northern Residents, Offshores and Bigg's ecotypes. Some have names, like Rhapsody (J32), Miracle and Nitinat (T12A). We have animals that were healthy and others with bone deformities (12844 and T171). Nitinat had serious tooth decay. Each one has a story to tell.

When a whale washes up today, Fisheries and Oceans Canada works

Orca specimens in the Royal BC Museum collection as of 2020.

Catalog #	Locality	Date	Sex	Ecotype
4555	Victoria	unknown	M	unknown
5106	Cherry Point	1944-09-28	F	unknown Resident
5214	Estevan Point	1945-07-04	F	unknown
5319	Estevan Point	1945-07-04	M	Offshore
5655	Quadra Island	1949-12-10	U	Northern Resident
6721	Reid Island	1949-10-04	U	Northern Resident
8386	Alert Bay	1973-08-07	M	unknown Resident
8861	Lasqueti Island	1975-03-10	M	unknown Resident
12844	Tofino	1976-04-09	M	Bigg's
9716	Strongtide Island, Oak Bay	1977-07-15	M	unknown Resident
10833	Nanaimo	1977-08-08	F	Miracle
16196	Discovery Island	1977-10-00	M	unknown Resident
10001	Boundary Bay	1979-01-18	M	Bigg's
10402	Bamfield	1981-06-23	U	Bigg's
16006	Port Renfrew	1986-08-17	F	Southern Resident
16630	Tsawassen	1986-10-00	U	unknown
16639	Ucluelet	1987-11-13	M	unknown Resident
16814	Barkley Sound	1989-04-11	M	Southern Resident
uncatalogued	Port Renfrew	2013-04-14	M	Bigg's
uncatalogued	Prince Rupert	2013-10-20	F	Bigg's (T171)
21465	Comox	2014-12-04	F	Southern Resident (Rhapsody J32)
uncatalogued	Comox	2014-12-04	F	Southern Resident (J32's foetus)
uncatalogued	Cape Beale	2016-09-15	M	Bigg's (Nitinat T12A)

Rhapsody's vertebrae lined up beside her skull to save space in the collection. RBCM photo.

with Indigenous communities to decide whether the body should remain for cultural reasons or whether it could be taken for science or display. In the winter of 2014, I received a call that an orca had died in the Courtenay/Comox area. This was my introduction to Rhapsody (J32) and her unborn calf. What followed was a frenzy of phone calls and emails to decide whether we had a budget to prepare a whale. Radio, newspaper and television reporters followed. As the person receiving Rhapsody and her calf's skeleton, I became captive in[side] the orca world.

It also was a rude awakening to hear that someone had snuck onto the beach hours before the necropsy and cut a handful of lower teeth from Rhapsody's lower jaw. Even more so when I learned that researchers had to dispose of her muscles and internal organs as toxic waste. Orcas eat what they were taught to eat, even if salmon and sea lions are contaminated. As apex predators, orcas accumulate industrial chemicals from the food chain throughout their lives. Lulu, who died in 2017 off Scotland, had contaminant levels 20 times higher than is considered safe or *manage-*

able. She died because of fishing gear, not industrial pollution, but she had never reproduced. One industry kept her from breeding. Another finished her off.

My role as a scavenger, acquiring orca skeletons for the museum collection, has increased in the last few years, with five animals recovered since 2013. This puts us back on par with historic collections in the 1940s, 1970s and 1980s, although there are 20-year gaps where no animals were acquired. These gaps reflect a number of factors: the fact that the museum has never had an orca specialist on staff, that preparation of whales is expensive, that their appearance on an accessible shoreline is hit and miss, and that we need dedicated space to clean skeletal material on such a large scale. Today the museum is extremely fortunate to have Michael deRoos and Michiru Main of Cetacea Inc. nearby to prepare whale material. They have prepared seven whales for the Royal BC Museum in the last decade, including the delicate skeleton of Rhapsody's foetus. Even without an orca specialist, we collect and maintain specimens to serve the larger scientific research community.

Specimens preserved in museum collections are invaluable sources of information for the study of wildlife, especially for animals like whales, which are hard to follow and may be rare in the wild. Museums are a time machine allowing researchers to study specimens collected decades or even

Bigg's orcas are at the top of the food chain and among the most contaminated animals in the world. Jared Towers photo.

hundreds of years ago. Obviously we don't go out shooting whales just to put them on a shelf. Instead, we rely on opportunistic collection of animals that died for one reason or another.

Why collect whales, or any specimen for that matter? A specimen collection is essentially a biological library, and each specimen is a book with its own story to tell. Stable isotopes locked in tissues help determine an organism's ecological position. Variation in tooth layers can show an animal's ecology changing through time. We can study disease in wildlife and extract pollutants to determine human

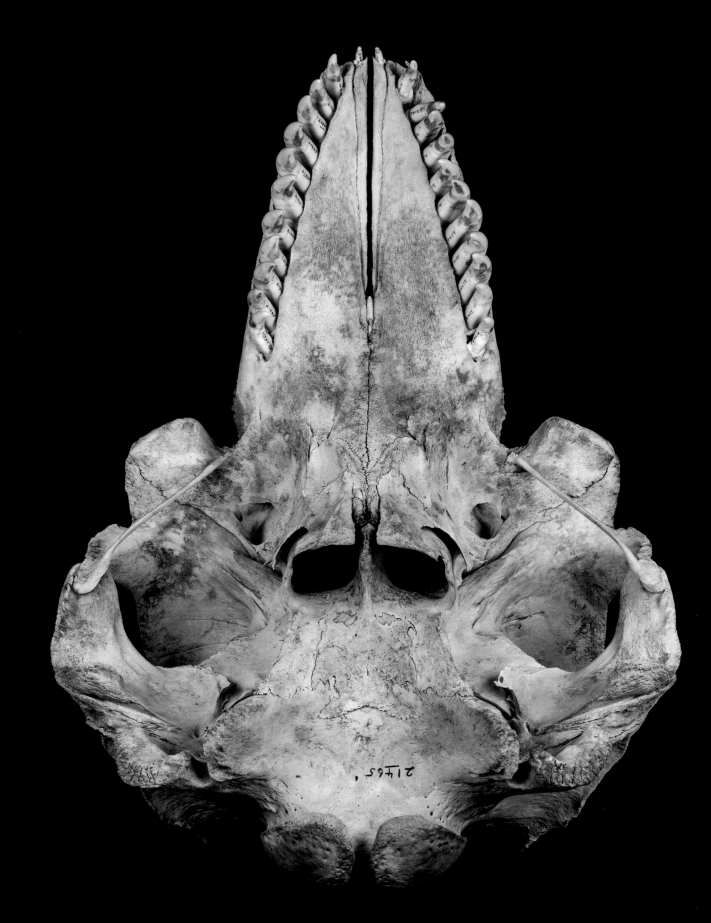

EACH ORGANISM IS UNIQUE TREASURE TROVE OF INFORMATION. EVEN THE PARASITE COMMUNITY IN AN ORCA CAN TELL YOU VOLUMES ABOUT ITS LIFESTYLE.

impacts on nature. DNA studies help determine population structure and interrelationships among species, and can be used to define species. Variations in anatomy, body systems and the geographic range of a species can all be studied from museum specimens. Each organism is a unique treasure trove of information. Even the parasite community in an orca can tell you volumes about its lifestyle. One hundred years ago, museum collectors had no idea how to study stable isotopes in ecology or DNA in population biology, but they collected specimens and made them available for study. Museums continue this practice today as a service to an unknowable future generation of scientists.

The acquisition of an orca is not without cost. Rhapsody and her foetus cost $11,625 to prepare. This figure doesn't reflect the volunteer effort and the in-kind support from Fisheries and Oceans Canada needed to get both animals off the beach. While it would be helpful to have dedicated funding in place to support whale collections, in reality, the decision to prepare

a whale is retroactive and quick. A whale on the beach attracts scavengers, and decay sets in rapidly. We prepare what we can afford on a case-by-case basis—such was the case for Nitinat. When his body was discovered, we could only afford to prepare his skull, not the entire skeleton.

Since orcas are on the larger end of the specimen spectrum, museums also have to consider how much space to allocate to a growing orca collection. Even a skull needs over a metre of shelf space. We save space by keeping skeletons disarticulated and performing our version of Tetris with the bones. Despite gaps in our holdings from 1950 to 1969 and 1990 to 2009, the Royal BC Museum has the largest collection of orcas along the entire Pacific coast of North America, and it's a destination for anyone doing specimen-based research on Pacific orcas.

As a museum curator along the Pacific coast, it's no surprise I ended up connected to orca research. Some say they were transformed by their encounters with orcas. I don't think my increased contact

A large Bigg's orca skull alongside that of a Northern Resident on open shelving in the RBCM collection. RBCM photo.

with orcas changed me. My connection to nature has always been there. I saw "happy orcas" in man-made ponds and witnessed my favourite swamp bulldozed to be replaced by a doughnut shop and a quick-lube outlet. In school, I was the odd one out, chasing snakes rather than a hockey puck. If I'd moved to the Pacific coast earlier, the scenery would have been different, but the outcome would have been the same. I probably would have had favourite tidepools rather than fish tanks, and I might have latched on to orcas sooner.

I lived through the heyday of orcas collected for live exhibit. Now, as part of the museum community, I continue to collect orcas to support scientific research. More importantly, my role as a connector has taken on renewed importance as I use tours, exhibits and online content to link museum visitors to science. People light up when they see and touch a skeleton, especially if they knew the animal. Emotions run high when people see Rhapsody's skeleton. It's hard not to find a personal connection in each animal's story.

What I've learned from orcas relates more to their dietary choices and to contaminants in the marine food chain. Thanks to Rhapsody, I chose to lower my trophic level to herbivore, and I gave up sport fishing. As a father of three, I see my girls growing up in a new era. Their first orca encounters were in the wild, not beside a pale blue aquarium pen. Children today are fed an ecological message at every turn, and thanks to science and a changing society, we are learning to tread lightly. So much has changed since I was a child heading to Marineland, riding in the back seat of a gas-guzzling 1971 Chevy Bel Air. People now are realizing that simple day-to-day choices impact nature, even things as large as a whale. Where we go from here, science and society, is entirely our decision. Anyone can make a difference. ⤳

Skeletons on movable shelving make the most use of limited space in a museum collection. RBCM photo.

Beginnings

Paul Spong

MY FIRST GLIMPSE OF AN ORCA was far from the ocean: a massive brain immersed in formalin in a huge glass jar on a bench in Dr. Pat McGeer's lab in the Kinsmen Laboratory of Neurological Research at the University of British Columbia. My immediate thought was "What on earth does this creature do with this brain?" I can still see it. The silky surface was covered in dark grey lines that represented convolutions in the cerebral hemispheres, the most recently developed parts of the brain and the areas responsible for its highest functions, things like memory, perception, thought. On the shelf above, there were several smaller jars with human brains in them. The brains were much smaller, obviously less developed, and looked puny in comparison. Wow!

The year was 1967. At the time I was a physiological psychologist, interested in the way brains work, and I had come to UBC to interview for a job that involved half-time neurological research on the campus and half-time behavioural research with a newly captured orca at the Vancouver Aquarium. I knew next to nothing about orcas, or cetaceans in general for that matter. About the closest I'd come was having a neighbour in New Zealand who owned Whale Island off the coast of Whakatane, where I grew up. The island had been a whaling station in the heydays of commercial whaling. By the time I arrived the whales were long gone, so my early life was no help. Fortunately, I was on the UCLA campus, where a prominent cetacean scientist, Dr. Ken Norris, was a professor of zoology. He generously gave me advice about research possibilities. Since orcas are the largest members of the dolphin family, and because much was already known about dolphin

(*Facing page*) ORCA SONAR **CHRIS VON SZOMBATHY**

Paul Spong with Skana at the Vancouver Aquarium. Photo courtesy Paul Spong.

gap. If she was correct, I tossed half a dead herring into the pool as a reward. Diana took a surprisingly long time to solve the initial one-or-two-lines problem, but once she got it, she was a willing performer. At one point I realized that she wasn't eating all the reward fish but instead was piling them up at a spot in the pool for later consumption. It got me thinking about motivation. The results showed that Diana's visual acuity underwater was about the same as a cat's in air, quite good but not great, and unsurprising in that her primary sensory modality as a dolphin was acoustic.

Moving on to Skana, I used a similar but more complicated procedure. The apparatus was a box with a plexiglass screen that kept her a standard distance away from the cards. Again, there were levers on either side of a partition, and Skana's task was to push up the lever on the side with the two-line card. This time, I tried to reduce the human element by controlling the experiment with logic circuitry located in my lab some

hearing, his suggestion was to look at vision. That's what I proposed, and it got me the job.

I began by looking at visual acuity with a dolphin named Diana. This was partly to sort out experimental procedures before I started working with the orca, Skana. I stationed an apparatus with two levers on either side of a partition in a "research" pool at the back of the aquarium and slipped cards with one or two vertical black lines into slots. Diana's task was to push up the lever on the side with two lines, the idea being to determine the point at which she was unable to distinguish the distance away. A doorbell signalled the beginning of a "trial." A "correct" response turned on a car headlamp, and a carousel fish feeder on the side of the pool dispensed half a dead herring as a reward. Like Diana, Skana took a long time to learn an initial visual discrimination, but once she "got it" was a consistent performer through literally thousands of trials. I ran the experiment in the early morning, before the public was admitted to the aquarium. A session consisted of 72 trials. Then one morning, having achieved 100 per cent correct responses on a problem in which the gap between the two lines was one-sixteenth of an inch, Skana suddenly, from one trial to the next, reversed her behaviour and began pushing up only the "wrong" lever. Not only that, she vocalized vigorously before and after pushing up the lever. This went on throughout the session and then for 4 more days, after which I took a break to think. My immediate and main conclusion was that Skana had said something to me, loudly and clearly: NO!

For the first time, I started thinking about Skana in terms of *who* she was. Up to that point, despite what I'd seen of an orca brain, I'd deliberately stayed clear of the line of thinking promoted by Dr. John C. Lilly, that dolphins are intelligent, sentient beings. Rather, I'd begun my work by treating Skana as if she were an unknown creature on the order of complexity of a laboratory rat and kept my thoughts distant. Now she had turned my head sideways, forcing a new perspective. I began by searching the behavioural literature for reports of similar sudden change. Finding none, I labelled Skana's behaviour a "spontaneous reversal" and again started thinking about motivation. Half a dead herring couldn't be much of a reward for an animal weighing thousands of pounds; besides, the task was so repetitive and the environment so barren that Skana had perhaps become bored to the point of rebelling.

I did two things at that point. One was to test if a non-food reward such as an activity like swimming around the pool or retrieving a ball might help recover the desired behaviour—not much. I then decided to find out if an acoustic reward could work. I wondered about this because quite clearly orcas are acoustic animals, and concrete tanks deprive their occupants of a normal acoustic world. At the time, the aquarium was holding a second orca in the research pool, away from public view. He was a young male, about two years old, who had been captured in Pender Harbour on the Sunshine Coast, north of Vancouver, in April 1968. I named him Tung Jen after hexagram 13 in the *I Ching*. He later became Hyak. The Chinese name means "fellowship with men." Given what I did to him, it was an odd choice. I was planning to work with him after Skana, and because I wanted a naïve second subject, had deliberately kept him isolated in the research pool. I instructed the care staff not to interact with him apart from feeding. Unknown to me until much later, some of the staff ignored my wishes and kept him company at times, so he did get a little attention. In any event, the upshot of my handling was that during the 9 months he had been held captive, the little guy had become sedentary and silent, floating quietly in one corner of the pool day and night, and moving only when fed.

To test the acoustic-reward hypothesis, I placed a loudspeaker in the bottom of a paint can, half submerged it in a corner of the pool, and ran wires into my lab next door, connecting the speaker to an amplifier, which in turn was connected to an acoustic waveform generator and a record player. I wanted to find out if an acoustic reward could be used to shape (that is, train) swimming behaviour. The cue to start a trial was a brief tone. I then waited for any movement consistent with swimming, and when that happened, turned on the reward sound. At first I played an assortment of various waveforms, but I soon settled on music as the reward. The results took my breath away. After just a couple of sessions, Hyak was swimming continuously around the pool, listening to music. The contrast with the slow pace of visual learning was remarkable. I was so impressed that I decided to abandon the swimming constraint

and reward anything that was not staying in the corner of the pool.

Under these conditions, Hyak's behaviour underwent a total transformation. He became an enthusiastic participant. As soon as I turned on the start tone, he would back out of his corner, turn and begin… something. It was a long list that included charging around the pool so fast that great waves sloshed over the sides; charging down one side then "porpoising" into the air and doing a barrel roll before diving back in; swimming upside down; swimming with his head in the air, slapping the water with his flukes as he swam; rolling over and over continuously, slapping the water with one pectoral fin and then the other. It soon became clear that his preference was for something new, music he hadn't heard before. One day he seemed to love listening to Ravi Shankar's sitar, so I decided to play the record for him again the next day. I turned on the signal tone, Hyak backed out of his corner, I turned on Ravi Shankar, he began to swim. Then, when only halfway down the first side, Hyak suddenly stopped and went back to his corner, remaining there until I put on new music. The explanation seemed pretty obvious. Hyak remembered that piece of Ravi Shankar's complicated music in such detail that he didn't need to hear it again. Unreal.

Another morning I decided to play Beethoven's Violin Concerto in D Major.

I cued the trial; Hyak started to back out of his corner; I turned on Beethoven. Sliding smoothly towards the middle of the pool, Hyak proceeded to arch his body so that his head was out of the water at one end and his flukes out of the water at the other. He then started to spray great fountains of water out of his mouth, gracefully waving his flukes as if conducting; slapping the water with his pectoral fin on one side, then rolling and doing it on the other side. His dorsal fin quivered constantly; all this in time to the music. Literally, he was dancing to Beethoven! I was transfixed, teary eyed, holding my breath watching. Then, thinking no one would believe me, I rushed off to find staff biologist Gil Hewlett and bring him to witness the incredible scene. I couldn't find Gil, and by the time I got back, Beethoven's music had ended, my room was silent and Hyak was floating quietly in the middle of the pool.

It is perhaps understandable that I too was being transformed at that time, witnessing scenes that convinced me I was dealing with no mere "animal" but a complex, highly evolved, sentient being. Moreover, I felt guilt because I had treated Hyak so badly. Realizing that I had deliberately kept myself distant, playing scientist and wearing a white lab coat, I decided to go back to Skana and get to know her. I developed a habit of going to the aquarium in the early morning, before any of the day staff arrived, sitting on a little training platform at the edge of Skana's pool and rubbing my bare feet over her head. She seemed to like that, sometimes rolling over so I could rub one side and then the other. When I played my flute to her, she seemed to like that too, floating stock still with her head out of the water. Clearly, she was listening. She let me walk out onto her back, taking me for a little ride and returning me to the platform. When I rang a little bell on the rung of a metal ladder in the pool, she turned upside-down underwater and pointed the front of her lower jaw at the source of the sound. This told me that she was listening to sound in the same way dolphins were known to hear. No surprise.

One morning, I stepped down to the training platform as usual and put my bare feet in the water while Skana floated at the other end of the pool. Sensing my presence, she roused and turned, heading slowly towards me on the surface. Then, when she was almost up to me and I was getting ready to greet her, she suddenly opened her mouth and slashed her jaws across my feet, so close that I could feel her teeth on the tops and bottoms of my feet. Naturally, and probably with a very slow reaction time because I was in an instant state of shock, I jerked my feet out of the water and sat trembling on the platform. Skana continued circling and resumed floating at the other end of the pool. After a considerable

IN THAT MOMENT, I REALIZED THAT SKANA WAS IN TOTAL CONTROL OF HER ACTIONS *AND*, WITH SUDDEN CLARITY, THAT I WAS NO LONGER AFRAID OF HER.

time, during which I calmed down enough to wonder why she had done that, I gingerly slipped my feet back into the water. Skana turned and headed slowly towards me on the surface, and again when she was almost to me, opened her jaws and slashed them across my feet so I could feel her teeth. Again I jerked my feet out of the water, terrified. It was a totally natural reaction, but now I started to wonder what was happening. Well, we went through this circle 10 or 11 times until finally, I was able to leave my feet in the water, relatively calmly, while she slashed her jaws across them. And then she stopped. In that moment, I realized that Skana was in total control of her actions *and*, with sudden clarity, that I was no longer afraid of her. She had swiftly and efficiently de-conditioned my fear of her. I came to regard that as a great gift from her to me, because I did not subsequently experience fear in her presence, and have not since experienced fear in the presence of other orcas. Simply put, she knew what she was doing, and I believe that other orcas know what they are doing, too.

What followed was more fast learning, and a hardening of my feelings about keeping orcas captive in concrete tanks. Among other fundamentals, I found out that orcas experience emotion, and that they have a sense of humour. The emotion lesson was a tough one, because it took the death of Skana's dolphin companion, Splasher, for me to understand it. Skana and Splasher used to chase each other around their pool, especially at night. It was a game, but one morning Splasher's lifeless body lay at the bottom of the tank. He had been crushed, probably against the side of the pool when Skana was chasing him. All that day and for several days after, billows of steam rose from Skana's head and the front of her pectoral fins. I was convinced that this was a sign of her intense regret at accidentally killing her friend. Later, as part of my effort to provide entertainment for Hyak, I brought my wife at the time, Linda, down to play her violin for him. Linda was a wonderful violinist. As she stood at the edge of his pool playing, Hyak came over and floated motionless below her with his head out of the water. As she played, wisps of steam rose from his head. For me, it was a sign that he loved Linda's music, and probably her, too. As for humour, I got it one morning when, as I was leaning out over Skana, a packet of cigarettes fell out of my shirt pocket into the water. It floated around on the surface, and I asked Skana to bring it back to me. Skana ignored it a first, but after awhile carefully grasped the packet in the front of her jaws and headed towards me. I reached out, and as I did so, she dunked the cigarettes under the water and handed me the pack. The cigarettes were soaked of course, and I got not just the joke but the point, though not being a quick study it took me years more to stop smoking.

As time passed, I became more and more convinced that keeping Skana and Hyak captive in concrete tanks was unfair, even cruel, in that it deprived them of the acoustic world they depend on, and also deprived them of the company of close kin. My opinions were not welcomed. After I announced at a UBC lecture summarizing my work that Skana should be allowed to return to her family in the ocean, I lost my job. I was devastated, but my life then took a course that led me to become an advocate for whales and to my home and work at OrcaLab on Hanson Island. No complaints, though I do have regrets.

My biggest regret is that that I lost the extraordinary opportunity I had to be close to Skana and Hyak, to learn more from them, and to do more for them. I wanted the Vancouver Symphony to perform for them at the aquarium, which I'm certain would have pleased crowds immensely, as well as the whales. It never happened, because of the wall that existed between my opinions and the aquarium's. Years later, some aquarium staff became my colleagues, which was nice, but the future was no help at the time.

I did have one more chance to play my flute for Skana. It came about in 1974 because of a request from *Time* magazine that had sent a reporter and photographer to Vancouver to do a story about Greenpeace's anti-whaling campaign. My comrade Bob Hunter and I were allowed into the aquarium to see Skana. I stepped down onto the training platform in the now much larger pool to play my flute for her. As she'd done so many times before, Skana floated quietly with her head out of the water below me, listening while I played. It was so nice, like coming home, and such a bittersweet moment. After me, Bob got down onto the platform, and when Skana came over, he started rubbing his hands over her head, thoroughly enjoying the opportunity. Skana seemed to enjoy the situation too, moving her head about so the long strands of Bob's hair gently caressed her. Then suddenly, Skana opened her jaws wide. Her intent was clear. Skana wanted Bob to put his head into her mouth. After hesitating briefly, Bob accepted the challenge. The moment changed his life.

I'll leave this account of beginnings with one more orca joke. It was 1972. A few of us had started a campaign to convince Canada to stop whaling. Farley Mowat had just published his book *A Whale for the Killing* and was in Vancouver on a cross-country

MY BIGGEST REGRET IS THAT THAT I LOST THE EXTRAORDINARY OPPORTUNITY I HAD TO BE CLOSE TO SKANA AND HYAK, TO LEARN MORE FROM THEM, AND TO DO MORE FOR THEM.

publicity tour. Probably because of my infamy, I was invited to a party at the Georgia Hotel, where I met Farley. We spent the evening sitting on the floor in a corner of the room, swapping stories and drinking beer, trying to figure out how to save the whales. Blurry bottom line was, if we could convince Canada, the world would follow. The next day I took Farley over to Victoria to visit Sealand of the Pacific, where a young male orca named Haida was held captive. I wanted Farley to meet a whale. Sealand was welcoming. A couple of years earlier they had allowed Canada's National Film Board to make a film, *We Call Them Killers*, about Haida and his young albino companion, Chimo, in which the flautist Paul Horn played for them. Haida became ill following Chimo's death, refusing food, and Paul's music was widely credited with helping him recover.

Sealand's rectangular pen was surrounded by ocean and enclosed by netting that had seaweed growing on it. Visitors were able to stand at the railing, looking down into the pool, and they got very close-up views of the whales. One of

Haida's favorite things to do with visitors was bring up a little piece of seaweed in his lips and present it to them. Haida did this with Farley several times, bringing up a piece of weed for him, with Farley placing it back on the front of Haida's head. Then, as Farley reached out once more, Haida opened his jaws wide, and the piece of seaweed fell into the back of his throat. Haida wanted Farley to reach down through his jaws and take the gift. Farley got it immediately and, gesturing with his hands, exclaimed "No Way!" An instant later, Haida retrieved the little piece of seaweed and presented it to Farley on the tip of his tongue. Point made on both sides.

A lot happened in the years that followed. Canada did stop whaling, the International Whaling Commission agreed to impose a moratorium on commercial whaling that still stands today, and though it is imperfect, in large measure the whales were saved, or at least they came back from the brink. My life has been blessed in so many ways, and without creating the list of the blessings that followed Skana, I shall ever be grateful. ～⁂

FALL HUNTING **APRIL BENCZE**

A Transient orca travels with their family through the tidal passages of the Xwe'malhkwu
(Hamalco) First Nation (around the Discovery Islands) east of Vancouver Island, 2016.
The orcas' presence marked the arrival of fall as they passed through, hunting the
rocky shoreline in search of seals and sea lions.

Killer Whales Who Changed the World

Mark Leiren-Young

WE'LL NEVER KNOW which orcas made waves for their communities beneath the surface, but here are six celebrity cetaceans who changed the way humans see—and treat—killer whales.

MOBY DOLL

THE FOUR-YEAR-OLD SOUTHERN RESIDENT ORCA was just off the coast of Saturna Island when he felt the harpoon hit the back of his neck. The metal pierced his skin, and the rope flipped around on itself into a loose knot. Whether it was the metal that hit and cracked the back of his skull or the pain from the wound, the young whale passed out, dropped below the water and began to drown. His mother dove to the rescue, along with another whale—likely his brother, since male orcas in this community stay close to their mothers. The two older whales caught the sinking child and lifted him to the surface.

We now know that orcas look after each other, but the humans who'd harpooned the young whale were shocked. Sculptor Sam Burich, who had fired the harpoon, had been told that killer whales were the most dangerous predator on the planet. If you believed the experts, the older whales should have been driven into a feeding frenzy and feasted on the young one.

It was June 16, 1964, and most humans were so afraid of killer whales that the idea of capturing one for display was almost unthinkable. Fishermen shot at them because orcas ate valuable chinook salmon. The military in Canada and the United States shot orcas for target practice. The Canadian government mounted a machine gun near Campbell River to eliminate the threat to their salmon and the tourism industry.

The Vancouver Aquarium had hired Burich to use an orca's body as a model for an anatomically accurate sculpture. They'd hired Ronald Sparrow, a Musqueam fisherman with his own harpoon gun, to kill their specimen. The men set up camp at East Point on Saturna Island—just on the Canadian side of the international border in the part of the Pacific Ocean known as the Salish Sea. When the orcas steered clear of the coast, Sparrow left to return to work, and Burich and his assistant, Joe Bauer, got custody of the harpoon.

As the larger orcas held their wounded podmate above the water, Bauer approached in a skiff and called to Burich that the whale was wounded, but he believed the injury was superficial and the orca could be saved and brought back to Vancouver.

Murray Newman, founding director of the Vancouver Aquarium, made the decision to take the orca home. CBC TV in Vancouver reported that the aquarium had captured "a monster."

Within days the "monster," dubbed Moby Doll, became Canada's biggest star. Although Bauer told his employers that he'd seen the orca's penis, they were certain he was mistaken. For several reasons—including the shape of the dorsal and the orca's friendly nature—"experts" were certain they'd captured a female.

The experts were wrong. Bauer was right.

Moby was initially held in a dry dock, where an estimated 20,000 people saw him on the one day the public was allowed to visit. A week later he was moved to a makeshift pen built by the Canadian military.

Although he lived less than three months thanks to the poor conditions of the water, Moby-Mania changed everything for orcas. Humans stopped seeing them as sea beasts and started seeing them as the ultimate aquarium exhibits.

Decades after his death, recordings of Moby's vocalizations revealed that he was a Southern Resident from J pod and confirmed that orca "language" is learned and passed down through generations.

Moby Doll's capture initiated the age of killer whale captivity.

His captivity also launched the careers of many orca scientists—including Dr. Michael Bigg, whose research ended orca captures in the Salish Sea when it showed that there was more than one type of orca and that the Southern Residents were endangered.

NAMU

THE TWO ORCAS were likely chasing salmon when the storm hit. Their echolocation allowed them to see the fish they were chasing, but not the net they were swimming into. The pair of Northern Residents from C1 pod—a 22-foot-long adult and a 10-foot-long juvenile—were trapped off the coast of Namu, British Columbia, just south of Bella Bella.

They could call to friends and family, but there was no chance of rescue. Echolocation doesn't work well at detecting holes in netting.

When the two fishermen arrived to take in their nets, they were shocked to discover what they'd caught. A year earlier they might have shot the predators, which they considered competitors for valuable salmon—but that was before crazy city people started saying they'd pay $20,000 or more for a live killer whale.

The next day Bill Lechkobit and Bob McGarvey went to the media, trying to spark a bidding war. They hooked several potential buyers from throughout North America until the younger whale—the one every aquarium wanted—slipped out of a hole in the net. They were prepared to cut the other orca loose when Seattle's Ted Griffin arrived with US$8,000 in cash. Griffin had an aquarium on the Seattle waterfront, and he'd raised the money by convincing the people running neighbouring businesses that a whale on display would turn the pier into the city's top tourist destination.

After buying the orca, which he named Namu, Griffin partnered with Don Goldsberry of the Tacoma Aquarium to deliver the prize in a floating pen. The media followed Namu's journey for 19 days. So did some of Namu's podmates. The whale's family—almost certainly his mother and siblings—followed, calling to Namu. The family finally turned back. We didn't know why at the time, but these were Northern Residents, and they wouldn't enter the territory of the Southern Residents.

When Namu arrived in Seattle's harbour on July 28, 1965, he was greeted by go-go dancers and a rock 'n' roll band. Five thousand paying customers met the orca on his first day in his new home.

Namu delivered on the promise of Moby Doll, proving that orcas were intelligent and friendly. Soon Griffin was riding Namu in the world's first-ever killer whale shows.

Namu launched songs and dances and a Hollywood movie by the writer who'd created the hit TV series *Flipper*, the story of a heroic dolphin. *Namu, the Killer Whale* was a family-friendly twist on Frankenstein, showing that these monsters were just misunderstood.

Namu died before the movie was released.

Less than a year after arriving in Seattle, Namu was poisoned by the harbour's polluted water. His necropsy revealed a bullet from a Springfield rifle—a gunshot wound from about a decade earlier. One-quarter of all killer whales caught for aquariums from the Salish Sea in the 1960s and 1970s had bullet wounds. We will never know how many orcas in the Pacific Ocean were killed by the guns of fishermen—and the US and Canadian military—before the capture era began.

Namu inspired Griffin and Goldsberry to invent the business of catching and selling killer whales. They sold the first orca they caught to SeaWorld, which named her Shamu—a combination of "She" and "Namu."

Shamu became the most famous orca in the world and the stage name for the stars of all SeaWorld shows for generations.

SKANA

K POD WAS TRYING TO ESCAPE the sounds of explosions and the boats that were chasing them. But the 15 orcas swam right into a net in Yukon Harbor in Washington State, herded by the humans dropping seal bombs (small explosives used to scare seals).

On February 15, 1967, the orcas swam around each other, desperately looking for a way to escape. Two trapped themselves in the mesh and drowned. The other orcas watched their podmates die, listened to their hearts stop, as the hunters above them examined their catch to determine who would be best to display.

Five were full-grown adults and were considered too large to display—and too heavy to ship. They were released.

Two were set aside for SeaWorld.

A 17-year-old orca was offered to the Vancouver Aquarium, but the director,

Murray Newman, didn't have a proper tank for a whale. If the Vancouver Aquarium wouldn't display a killer whale in Vancouver, the Seattle Aquarium would. They sent the whale they named Walter to the Vancouver Boat Show as a temporary exhibit.

Walter was a sensation, and the Vancouver Aquarium agreed to buy him. Soon after Walter's arrival the aquarium team discovered that he was a she. A radio contest was held to choose a new name, and the winning suggestion came from a six-year-old boy, Peter Payne, who proposed the name "Skana." This was both the Haida name for killer whale and the name of his father's boat.

Skana became a cetacean superstar, and everyone who came to Vancouver wanted to meet her—including Prime Minister Pierre Trudeau.

Newman wanted to make sure that if the Vancouver Aquarium had an orca, they'd learn about her. The revolutionary decision to hire a neuroscientist resulted in world-shaking out-of-the-tank thinking.

Paul Spong was testing Skana's intelligence when he became convinced that she was testing his (see pages 133–140). As he worked with Skana, he declared that she and her relatives should be known as "orcas" based on their Latin name, *Orcinus orca*. He said that humans should only call Skana's kin "killer whales" if we were prepared to refer to ourselves as "killer apes."

THE EVOLUTIONARY THEORY KNOWN AS THE GRANDMOTHER HYPOTHESIS POSITS THAT FOR HUMANS—AND A FEW MARINE MAMMALS LIKE ORCAS AND SHORT-FINNED PILOT WHALES— WISDOM IS MORE VALUABLE THAN REPRODUCTIVE ABILITY.

Spong was soon fired and became the most influential early anti-captivity activist. After his dismissal, Spong was often seen outside the aquarium, holding a protest sign and demanding Skana's release. Thanks to Spong, Vancouver became the heart of the anti-captivity movement and the global effort to save the whales.

Because of his experiences with Skana, Spong convinced a small Vancouver anti-nuclear organization to hit the high seas to combat whalers. Spong didn't launch Greenpeace, but he turned it green, shifting the organization's focus to environmental issues. As he helped lead the fight against whaling around the world, Spong would tell people, "We're working for Skana. We're her ambassadors. She wants out, and wants her people to be free."

Skana died at the Vancouver Aquarium on October 5, 1980.

GRANNY

THE YOUNG FEMALE ORCA who would one day become known as Granny began exploring the Pacific Ocean when chinook were huge and abundant. The waters weren't pristine, but they hadn't become a toxic dumping site for chemicals that would never disappear. Large ships were rare, huge tankers nonexistent.

When the Center for Whale Research in Friday Harbor, Washington, began estimating the ages of the Southern Resident orcas, they knew Granny (or J2) was old, but no one knew how old. They believed it had been decades since she'd reproduced, and Granny was always seen with Ruffles, who everyone assumed was her son. Her birth year was guesstimated at 1911.

This would mean Granny hit the high seas just before the *Titanic* did.

Orcas are one of the only species besides humans where females experience menopause, a prolonged life beyond their reproductive years. The evolutionary theory known as the grandmother hypothesis posits that for humans—and a few marine mammals like orcas and belugas and narwhals—wisdom is more valuable than reproductive ability.

Orcas are a matriarchal society, and the matriarchs are vital to their survival.

Granny's presumed age didn't become controversial until after the anti-captivity movie *Blackfish* was released in 2013 and her longevity was used to attack SeaWorld, where employees regularly claimed that captive orcas lived longer than wild whales.

Suddenly, the idea that Granny might be a hundred had political implications. How old was she?

Tests on Ruffles showed that he was not her son, but didn't prove how old Granny was or wasn't. Ruffles's story had another surprise plot twist. Not only wasn't he Granny's son, but the whale known as J1 wasn't a member of J pod. Ruffles was from L pod.

When Granny died in 2016, she was world famous as "the hundred-year-old whale." Whether she was a hundred or not, she wasn't a youngster. The scientists at NOAA (the US National Oceanic and Atmospheric Administration) estimated she was at least in her 80s.

In Washington State there's a street named after her, and she was elected honorary mayor of Orcas Island.

However old Granny was, her age doesn't provide anything resembling definitive proof of how long an orca can live.

Orcas in the Salish Sea carry a higher toxic load than almost any other marine mammals in the world. Humans have over-fished chinook—the primary food source

Clint Rivers photo. Chris Young design.

of the Southern Residents—to the verge of extinction. And the polluted waters are a major shipping route, which makes it difficult for orcas to hear to hunt.

Meanwhile, there are orcas in other oceans where the water is cleaner and the food they eat is still plentiful. Some of the longest-lived marine life in the world lives in northern waters. Bowhead whales are known to live over 200 years. Greenland sharks can live over 400 years. So whether Granny was 80 or 100 or 150, she may not have qualified as an elder in oceans where there may still be matriarchs old enough to have been Granny's granny.

TILIKUM

THE TWO-YEAR-OLD ORCA CALF swimming in the frosty ocean off the coast of Iceland never saw the net. Neither did his mother or the other orca with him, possibly his sister. Echolocation, the sense orcas use to navigate the world, doesn't know how to process nets. This may be why orcas, who can fly through the air, never jump over nets to escape.

The young orca, who would become infamous as Tilikum, was one of the last whales captured by Don Goldsberry—the king of orca captures, who had pioneered rounding up and delivering orcas to marine parks.

Tilikum was delivered to a concrete holding tank in Saedyrasafnid, Iceland, before he was flown across the world to Canada. He joined two more Icelandic orcas as the stars at Sealand of the Pacific—a tiny marine park in Victoria, BC.

Sealand of the Pacific may not have been the all-time worst facility where a killer whale was ever displayed, but it ranks near the bottom of the list. The net pen was small, shallow (less than 20 feet deep) and shared by three orcas. And the whales were forced to sleep (or at least attempt to sleep) in a tiny holding pen because of fears that activists might try to liberate them. While it's rare for orcas to attack each other in the wild, the female orcas in Tilikum's tank were frequently raking him with their teeth.

While his home at SeaWorld has been compared to whale jail, his home in Sealand was orca Guantanamo. In 1991, after Tilikum and the other two orcas killed 21-year-old trainer Keltie Byrne, he was sold to SeaWorld, where he became their number-one orca stud, siring multiple orcas who would perform in Shamu shows.

In 1999, a 27-year-old man broke into SeaWorld and snuck into the orca pool. Tilikum presumably drowned him. He definitely castrated him. Staff arrived to see Tilikum displaying the body on his back.

In 2010, Tilikum attacked and killed his trainer, Dawn Brancheau, at SeaWorld Orlando.

Some orca experts believed that after all of his experiences—including his career as a sperm donor—Tilikum was psychotic. It's hard to believe he was a happy orca.

His story was told in the 2013 documentary *Blackfish*, a movie that changed the world's view of captivity and led marine parks, including SeaWorld, to end or at least commit to ending killer whale shows.

Tahlequah with her calf, summer 2018. Taylor Shedd of Soundwatch photograph, NMFS #21114.

Tilikum died at SeaWorld in 2016 at the age of 36, but thanks to *Blackfish*, he became the symbol for the anti-captivity movement.

TAHLEQUAH

A BABY GIRL. The mother orca looked at her daughter and, thanks to her sense of echolocation, knew her baby wasn't healthy. She knew the breathing was too shallow, the heartbeat too weak. After swimming off Clover Point, near Victoria, for less than an hour, the beautiful little orca gasped her last and the mother, known to humans as Tahlequah, dove to catch the body. Like so many mother orcas before her, Tahlequah set out to show her dead calf to her family, J pod.

Perhaps Tahlequah planned to show the body to the other pods as well, at a gathering of the clans humans call a superpod. Instead, she showed her daughter to the world, in what became known as a tour of grief.

The 20-year-old Southern Resident carried and cradled her daughter's body for 17 days as the world's media shared the story with a mix of fascination, horror and guilt. Whether Tahlequah was talking to us or not, her message was clear: we did this.

Some people claimed other orcas helped her carry her daughter, or they delivered food so the grieving orca could eat. We don't know. But what we do know is that she didn't drop her calf, and she didn't lose weight. So the idea that Tahlequah had help from her family seems more plausible than the possibility that she didn't sleep or eat for over two weeks, but didn't lose weight or sink from exhaustion.

Thanks to Tahlequah's epic tour, the American and Canadian governments worked together with the Lummi Nation and a mix of organizations with varying views on captivity to try to rescue and rehabilitate one of Tahlequah's podmates, Scarlet. The spunky three-year-old orca was starving, and because the world was watching, attempts were made to diagnose and treat her. It was a classic case of too little, too late. Warnings were sounded—and ignored—prior to Tahlequah stealing the media spotlight. But the idea of cross-border cooperation and marine park veterinarians working with anti-captivity organizations raised the possibility that humans could put their own politics aside to fight for the orcas.

Tahlequah's tour set the stage for a new approach to saving the endangered Southern Resident orca population. The following year Washington governor Jay Inslee proposed putting over one billion dollars into orca recovery, and the Canadian government declared they'd spend at least $200 million to help save the Southern Residents.

In 2019, the month of June, which had long been known as Orca Awareness Month in Canada and the United States, was renamed Orca Action Month.

Tahlequah accomplished what generations of human orca advocates couldn't. She shamed politicians into action. It remains to be seen whether her message was received in time. ⤳

Orcie the Orca

WRITTEN BY **the students of Oak and Orca School**

THIS STORY AND THESE IMAGES were created by the students of the Oak and Orca Bioregional Forest School, a program within a non-profit school that operates at P'KOLS on W̱SÁNEĆ (Saanich), Lekwungen (Songhees) and Wyomilth (Esquimalt) territory. We are a K–8 inter-age program seeking to provide community-based bioregional education that connects curriculum learning areas to imaginative and inquiry-based learning.

Throughout the past year and a half, we have done hands-on workshops and read stories about the kelp forests, sea life in intertidal zones, salmon life cycles, Coast Salish cultural connections to the Salish Sea, and perspectives on how industrial processes are impacting these ecosystems and, specifically, the Southern Resident orcas.

These art pieces emerged out of an inquiry art project we began at the beginning of April 2019. For four workshop sessions, a mentor set up a table with watercolours, ocean field guides and story books. They invited the students to make art inspired by questions: What is your relationship to the ocean and orcas? What do you want to people to know about the ocean and orcas? Why is the health of the ocean important? Many students expressed that they don't really know what their relationship to the ocean and orcas is or could look like, but also that they wanted to explore this question further.

From these lessons, one of my favourite student quotes was from eight-year-old T.: "The health of the ocean is important because the ocean is our life support system. No ocean, no us." This project was an invitation to our community to think deeper about our relationship to the Salish Sea and the Southern Resident orcas; it will continue to guide and shape our learning and our connection to place into the future. ∼➢

Orcie the orca
loves to swim

Play in the waves
with all their kin

Orcie the orca
hunts in a pod

If found alone
that would be odd

go to the ocean
take a look Orcie
the orca is chasing
a big chinook

Do you hear
the orcas' song?
They're telling us
there's something
wrong

They're telling us
there's not enough fish
A healthy ocean is
their greatest wish

Next time you stand
by the ocean blue
remember that
you're part of the
ecosystem too

Gillian McDonald, Oak Adams, Malcolm Blackburn and Ezra Gitberg

Above: Malcolm Blackburn, age 8; Below: Tashen Ao-Reeve, age 8

I am from the sea
I have seen you
Can you see me?

Clockwise from top left: Gillian McDonald (teacher); Oak Adams, age 9; Jamie Black, age 37; Ezra Gitberg, age 9; Catie Bainbridge, age 28

Learning to Live with Whales

Alex Morton

THE YOUNG FEMALE ORCA rested lightly on the bottom of the circular tank. Milk flowed from her swollen mammaries as she repeated the same vocalization over and over for the third day. The call had become a guttural croaking, so different from the melodic calls that had drawn me to spend my life trying to decipher the calls that orcas make. As dawn streaked the southern California sky, Orky, the father of the absent baby whale, called out… *piiituuuu*. I didn't expect his mate to answer.

My hydrophone had captured the shocking silence left behind as the starving baby was hoisted out of the tank. Corky hurled herself against the tank sides. She slammed the platform where humans commanded her in exchange for fish, then she sank to the bottom and began her lament for the baby she ached for.

This time she answered, *piiituuuu*, and rose to Orky's side. I straightened from my slumped position. Exhaustion evaporated. Something was happening. This was a brief crack in the barrier of understanding between two very different species, a moment where learning can occur. The two whales called, *piiituuuu*, *piiituuuu*, back and forth for 65 minutes, swimming side by side, their blowholes opening at the same instant, sucking air into their lungs simultaneously in the most intimate orca declaration: *we are family*. Later that morning Corky accepted the first food since she had lost her daughter.

This was the third baby that Corky, daughter of A23 of the A5 pod of the Northern Resident orca clan, had lost. The people entrusted with her care had risked their lives trying to position the baby on her mammaries in hopes she would learn to nurse. Corky was an attentive mother, but the circular tank meant she had to push her baby constantly away from the

USING OLD PHOTOS TAKEN AT THEIR CAPTURE, I FOUND THEIR FAMILY IN THE WILD AND I WENT TO LIVE IN THEIR HABITAT. I HAVE NOT FORGIVEN MYSELF FOR THIS BETRAYAL. IT SHOULD HAVE BEEN THE CAPTIVE WHALES AND NOT ME WHO MADE THIS JOURNEY.

wall. There was no opportunity for Corky to glide in a straight line and present her underside, where the life-sustaining milk could be found, to her daughter. The whale handlers hoped to return the baby to her mother once they got they her to accept tube feedings, but she died.

I sat tank-side for every birth. I spent over 600 hours a year recording the sounds and behaviours of these two whales, taken from BC waters in 1968 and 1969 when they were youngsters. I wanted to study how a baby whale learns its language, but with this death I finally saw the obvious. I might as well be studying human vocalizations of people separated from their parents when they were five and held in a room with no windows. There was nothing but tragedy and suffering to see here.

I was a young woman in my early 20s, determined to end the silence between my species and non-humans by cracking orca communication. In my singular pursuit of that knowledge, I turned my back on the captives. Using old photos taken at their capture, I found their family in the wild, and I went to live in their habitat. I have not forgiven myself for this betrayal. It should have been the captive whales and not me who made this journey.

In August 1980, a filmmaker approached my basecamp on Hansen Island, British Columbia, asking if I would agree to be filmed as I viewed the whales via his partner's underwater camera. The camera was fixed to the sea floor at a beach where we were just learning that the orca loved to rub. As I sat on the black-pebbled beach the next day, irritated to be wasting the day on land, a man emerged from the water and peeled off everything, revealing an Indigenous orca design tattooed on his shoulder. In less than a year, I was married to filmmaker Robin Morton, and we were living on a boat and expecting a baby.

In October 1984, we followed Scimitar's family, the A12s, into Fife Sound and ended our search for the perfect place to study whales. It was the Broughton Archipelago, Musg̱amagw Dzawada̱'enux̱w

Territory. There were whales, calm waters and a tiny one-room school serving the floathouse community of Echo Bay. Modelling my work after Dr. Jane Goodall, where the researcher goes to the animal rather than bringing the animal to the researcher, Robin and I learned more every day that we encountered the whales, particularly in the winter months.

The archipelago was A clan territory. They used it to hunt for the once-abundant overwintering chinook salmon, and for sleeping during the big summer orca gatherings that are essential to maintaining their culture. They entered the inlets on the ebb tide, like wolves hunting downwind. In the winter months, these fish-eating orca broke down into their smallest divisible units, mom and the kids. Hoping to make the longest possible uninterrupted recordings, I positioned myself far in front of the males, but I quickly learned the pods weren't following the males. The males hunted in less productive habitat, leaving the rich shorelines to the females and young whales. It was the oldest females who set the course.

I learned early on that the most important thing to whales is family. The loss of his mother is enough to kill an adult male, and I went on to learn more about the call *piiituuu*. It felt like a key.

When a pod came to an intersection, this call dominated sound production. As with Orky and Corky, wild whales often used it at the beginning and end of conversations. It also spiked during a birth witnessed in 1981.

What was the common thread that linked all these behaviours? Questions like this are what make science so much fun. After much thought, I wondered: was it the act of synchrony that linked all these activities to this call? In each instance, all participating whales were focused on the same thing: turning left or right, starting a duet or surrounding a labouring mother. Synchrony is deep-seated in orcas. Their survival depends on it. Baby whales must learn not to breathe when they are underwater, and so swimming in unison with their mother, they learn to open their blowhole that the same moment as mom. The iconic image of a line of whales with breath hanging in the air is a family portrait.

Other calls swept back and forth between adult sisters as they split the family to forage opposite sides of a channel with their youngsters. I interpreted these calls to mean, "I am over here and doing fine." However, researchers at Woods Hole suggested that the whale's highly sophisticated ear/brain connection, a superhighway compared with our auditory bike path, might be able to decipher acoustic holes punched out of the calls, minute attenuations of specific frequencies to decipher images. They might be able to "see" a school of fish between the whale making the sound and the whale receiving the sound. Are whale calls search beams of sound penetrating the darkness of the ocean?

It was the exquisite sensitivity of their hearing that forced them to abandon the Broughton Archipelago. Acoustic harassment devices installed by the newly arrived salmon farming industry to repel marauding seals produced a chirping noise so loud that I could hear it through the hull of my boat: 198 decibels, as loud as a jet engine at take-off. I witnessed each family of whales encounter the devices and avoid the region for 25 years. In October 2019, one family visited, and hopefully it will return. The other orca society on the BC coast, those that eat mammals and not fish, called Bigg's whales, abandoned the salmon highways where the farms were sited for the channel my house was floating in, and thus kept an island between themselves and the noise from the farms.

I wasn't sure what to do. I contacted the authorities. This was a violation of Canadian law, but the authorities were not interested in investigating. I published a scientific paper on displacement of whales by these sounds, and still government did nothing. As I waited for the whales to return, months and then years went by, and I wondered, *should I leave too?*

Robin would have known what to do, but he drowned in 1986 while using a rebreather, diving equipment that does not produce bubbles. He thought the lack of bubbles, which are a threat-gesture for whales, would allow him to get closer to them.

The orca matriarchs that last fished Kingcome Inlet have died during the 25-year exile of their families. Was the knowledge of how to fish this place sequestered out of reach, in a non-whale brain—mine? If I leave, no one will know they belong here, to make sure they can return. Can people bring ecosystems back into balance, if no one knows how the pieces fit?

I have spent the past three decades engaged in science, law and activism to move the salmon farming industry out of the archipelago into tanks on land. I do this to reopen the door to the whales who belong here. We have tried to protect parts of the earth by establishing parks to keep ourselves out, but today our survival hinges on learning how to live on this planet. We must use what we know to dovetail into the natural systems that power our world and learn to be good neighbours to the others we share this planet with. ⌒⤸

EBB TIDE AT SPRINGER POINT **TAVISH CAMPBELL**

Okisollo Channel, BC, 2012.

J-35

Gary Geddes

Do animals cry? she asks.
I don't know, I say, but I think

they grieve. I'd read about a camel
that sniffed her dead offspring

for days and wouldn't move
until they placed its pelt on her

back. Why do you ask? Her hand
on the breakfast counter looks tiny

beside mine. A milk-ring graces
her mouth, a toasted bread-crumb

clings to her cheek. A sympathetic
smile is all I have to offer.

J-35, she says, scarcely audible.
The orca in the news has carried

her dead calf for fourteen days,
trying to keep it above water,

travelling hundreds of miles
as J-pod forages for the scarce

spring salmon. When it isn't
resting on her head she grips

its tail with her teeth. J-35 knows
her baby's dead, she whispers;

I think she's trying to tell us
something. I leave the science

out for now: the most polluted
mammals on earth, the slurry

of toxins female orcas slough off
on their newborns. Extinction

looming, salmon stocks
depleted. Tanker traffic, the

old whale-road the Vikings
celebrated now a web of dirty

shipping lanes, booming
grounds, plastic archipelagos.

I think you're right, I say;
let's see what we can do. ∽➋

(Facing page) PRIDE **LAUREN BREVNER AND NEXW'KALUS-XWALACKTUN JAMES HARRY**

Luna the Lonely Political Whale

Briony Penn

IN **2004,** a documentary called *Web-Cam Girls* chronicled the rise of this new business model as the advent of web cameras inaugurated an era of online voyeurism. One of the women in the film, called Ana, confessed that the business was lonely and that she identified with the lonely whale up in British Columbia. The thing she most wanted to do was to get out of New York, fly to Gold River and touch Luna. Ana was not alone. Millions had heard about Luna the Lonely Whale, and he became a symbol of our collective longing for clan, connection and place. Found alone in Muchalat Inlet, near Gold River, off the west coast of Vancouver Island in 2001, Luna had become separated from his pod of Southern Resident killer whales (SRKWs), who typically reside over the summer in the Salish Sea. For a world hungry for family reunions, Luna unleashed a second Fraser River of emotion draining into this embattled region, through which the endangered J, K and L pods have had to navigate. Ever since 1964, when a group from the Vancouver Aquarium, who had gone to harpoon a whale, witnessed the raising up of a wounded Moby Doll (a male juvenile from L pod) to the surface of the water by his family, our connection to the whales has grown to encompass an astonishing array of human longings, followed by political opportunism. Whether leading parades against pipelines or pilgrimages for petting whales, the SRKWs are the political hot potatoes of the coast: too hot to touch, and none hotter than Luna.

The dock at Gold River was a challenging place, but the most likely place for the Anas of the world to see the lonely whale. It's at the end of a long gravel road next to an abandoned pulp mill that was dropped into Mowachaht/ Muchalaht First Nation territory to service an industry that had left the region devastated. The dock was where a media circus camped out for 10 days

Luna nudges private watercraft at Gold River and visits people eager to see an orca up close, 2003. Scott Eklund photo.

in 2004 to report on L98's proposed capture and relocation to his pod in the Salish Sea by the federal Department of Fisheries and Oceans and the Vancouver Aquarium. L98 is the number assigned by whale researchers to the young male in the L2 matriline of L pod. Also known as Tsu'xiit (pronounced Tsukeet) by the Mowachaht/Muchalaht, L98 became the most politicized whale in British Columbia's industrial history. As Canada headed into an election that year, our national commmitments like protecting endangered species and observing Indigenous rights to key resources like salmon were in a poor state of repair—kind of like the dock. The politicization of the

whale was inevitable, but few of us knew how political it would get.

The news frame for the story was constructed on the assumption of a problem, articulated by our national broadcaster as "Luna's dangerous predilection for the company of humans." The question unasked was, dangerous to whom? Luna was found at a young age near Yuquot, where Muchalat Inlet opens into Nootka Sound. He may have got separated from his family during one of their increasingly desperate searches for depleted chinook salmon off the west coast. As far as scientific understanding of whales goes (about 50 years of research), a whale leaving its

PRESSURE ALSO CAME FROM INDUSTRIAL INTERESTS—THE FISH FARM INDUSTRY WANTED FEWER OBSTACLES BETWEEN THEIR PRODUCT AND MARKET. TWO THINGS STOOD IN THEIR WAY: THE MOWACHAHT/ MUCHALAHT FIRST NATION AND A PESKY WHALE CALLED TSU'XIIT.

pod is unusual. Males usually stay with their maternal clan for life, only a very few becoming breeding males within the larger Resident population. Something happened to L pod that winter, with several members going missing, and Tsu'xiit emerged alone in the sound. The "problem" then became Luna habituating to human company— boats, float planes, visitors to the dock and increasingly, fish farms, as they started to multiply around Muchalat Inlet.

Some members of the public were persauded by the idea of capture and relocation. The popular movie *Free Willy*, and an earlier successful reunion of the two-year-old Springer with his Northern Resident killer whale pod in 2002, had set the scene for Luna. To see the whale reunited with its pod was appealing, de-spite the impractical plan of reintroducing him when the pod was in Puget Sound, where there is intense summer traffic. Locals from Gold River, used to living with wildlife and enjoying the boom in tourism, called it life and shrugged their shoulders. The DFO, with an obligation to uphold a federal law that said you can't pet a wild whale and a public that wanted to pet a

whale who liked being petted, was less laissez-faire. After two years of a wait-and-see approach, politics prevailed, and the DFO was pressed into action. The money to capture Luna came from a variety of strange bedmates: well-meaning individ-uals from across North America, people like Ana, aquariums lining up for a sound investment should Luna not be accepted by his pod. Freedom of Information requests later revealed that Luna was destined for Marineland in Niagara Falls, ostensibly to be protected from himself. Pressure also came from industrial interests—the fish farm industry wanted fewer obstacles between their product and market. Two things stood in their way: the Mowachaht/ Muchalaht First Nation and a pesky whale called Tsu'xiit.

Tyee Ha'wilth Chief Mike Maquinna, a descendant of the chief who had greeted Captain Cook at Yuquot in 1778, had gone through a three-year process to stop the placing of new open-net fish farms in Mowachaht/Muchalaht territory, also under the jurisdiction of the DFO. The Mowachaht/Muchalaht's concerns were ignored, and they had taken up the challenge in the Supreme Court of British Columbia. The nation had good reason to stand by Tsu'xiit. During a long council meeting dealing with DFO negotiations, Mike Maquinna's father, the late Chief Ambrose Maquinna, had said that when he passed away he would come back as a kakawin (killer whale) to annoy the fish farms. Three days after he died, Tsu'xiit turned up near Yuquot. Luna's unreported "dangerous predilection" turned out to be for fish farms, which were a far bigger issue for the Mowachaht/Muchalaht than a small whale bothering boats. The fish farms were a long-term threat to the wild chinook, the salmon that had sustained the orcas and their people for thousands of years. Their survival depended on salmon, and Tsu'xiit was both a relative and a symbol of what was about to be lost.

By June of 2004, the DFO had issued permits for the fish farms, and TV cameras might have caught the flash of one of the eight new aluminum net pens belonging to Norwegian giant Grieg Seafood being installed up the inlet, including at the mouth of one of the richest chinook-bearing streams in Mowachaht/Muchalaht territory. Over the next 10 days, those of us on the docks experienced one of the most amazing, creative, mysterious and moving acts of civil disobedience that newspeople have ever missed. Mike Parfit of the Smithsonian Institute, who went on to make two films of Tsu'xiit with his partner Suzanne Chisholm, remarked that in 40 years of

making documentaries he had never seen anything like it. The events of the fortnight played out like a bizarre game of capture the flag, except the flag was a whale. DFO would go in their boats, find Luna and lure him down to their pen, and Mowachaht/Muchalaht canoeists, braving big seas and strong winds, would lure him over to the canoes and back up the inlet to Nootka Sound—some 20 to 30 kilometres away—with their singing and drumming. Fishing boats joined in to relieve the paddlers after long days on the sea. Day after day this repeated.

The DFO brought to the docks of Gold River a travelling circus of net pens, cranes, boats, scientists, PR people and enforcement officers. The media followed with cameras, wires, lights and truckloads of reporters and cameramen. The Mowachaht/Muchalaht stood firm with their own small armada of canoes and fish boats. What went unreported was the arrival of Grieg Seafoods with their own travelling road show of net pens, cranes, boats, fish-farm workers and farmed Atlantic salmon. The late Hereditary Chief Jerry Jack joked, "We should have sent Captain Cook back to his pod two hundred years ago; it would have saved a lot of problems." During the nine-day stand off, Jack had indicated to the DFO, "You move the fish farms out, and we'll talk about the whale." It was a fair statement, as the DFO had one department that promoted aquaculture and another that promoted the protection of the ocean. It was then, and remains now, a confused organization that puts impossible demands on its staff to deliver consistent messages and coherent policy. The media, of course, were only interested in the lonely whale story.

On the ninth evening, the DFO lured Luna into one of the farm pens after getting past the paddlers who were taking refuge in the lee of an island during heavy winds. Television reporters left Gold River in convoys for Campbell River to file the story that Luna the lonely whale was soon to be reunited with his pod—but they left too soon. The entire village, including Ambrose Maquinna's widow and granddaughter, came down to the dock to sing Maquinna's paddle song and bring Tsu'xiit back. Those of us who stayed joined in, pounding paddles on the weathered planks of that dock to drum him over from across the bay. We all watched, transfixed, as the whale broke through the line of DFO nets and boats and swam to the canoeists. That midsummer's night, with the sun sinking down, the flotilla accompanied Tsu'xiit back up the inlet to his ancestral village at Yuquot. The motley band of canoeists, women, men and children, wet, cold, exhilarated and exhausted, paddled past the tangled trappings of the DFO, fish farms and the international press, then disappeared over the horizon.

Chief Maquinna issued a request that evening asking for DFO to stop their attempts to capture the whale and to use the money for the capture to start a stewardship program led by his people. The next day, the DFO charged an Indigenous fisherman for interfering with the capture of Luna. The day after that they agreed to stop the capture and talk. Eventually a stewardship program was launched, and Luna was guarded by Mowachaht/Muchalaht watchmen until 2006, when he was accidentally killed by the prop of a large tug. Chief Jack was also killed that year, when his canoe overturned during a Tribal Canoe Journey—the loss of an important voice for the salmon, the orcas and the well-being of the nation. The fish farms continued to proliferate.

Today, wherever there are fish farms, chinook have continued to decline, to the point where most populations are on the brink of extinction. The SRKWs have gone from 84 in 2004 to 73 in 2019. The cause of decline is multivariate, but it is accurate to say they are starving to death. The population has little chance of recovery unless they can find more food. Fish farming is a major factor implicated in the demise of populations of salmon, and just as importantly, of chinook's primary food, herring. Despite decades of court cases, enquiries and scientific evidence, the removal of fish farms has been glacially slow. The first step to remove 17 fish farms from the Broughton Archipelago, on the other side of Vancouver Island from Gold River, only became operational in 2019.

Since Luna, the world has turned its gaze to other members of the SRKWs, most

Luna was known to spy-hop and touch people—and dogs. 2003. Scott Eklund photo.

an age where so many lives are displayed online, the emaciated bodies of whales are streamed alongside those of web-cam girls. The world watches, wondering if they are the harbingers of our own future.

This population now represents the most important political and legal obstacle to the expansion of the Trans Mountain pipeline and its accompanying tankers, and by association represents our political willingness to break our reliance on fossil fuels and address climate change. It is a testimony to these amazing animals that they continue to reach deep within our intellect and hearts, touching us on the contemporary issues most central to our survival. The whales are telling us what is wrong with our current system, whether it is decline from hunger, noise, disconnection, loss of biodiversity, industrial resource extraction, climate change, toxicity or even lonliness. The whales are also pointing us to an alternate worldview, one that has welcomed strangers to the land and recognizes the natural world as an essential element in every aspect of our lives—our livelihoods, our spirituality and ultimately our survival. ⮑

recently J35, who carried the dead body of her newborn calf for 17 days in the summer of 2018 and became an international symbol of their plight. There hadn't been a successful birth in the population for over three years, and all research pointed to the same factors: low chinook populations, accumulated toxicity in their fat and milk (which lowers the chance of survival in newborns), and rising noise levels. Already struggling to find salmon, the whales' stress is exacerbated by the increasing noise of boat and tanker traffic, which disrupts their echolocation and thus their cooperative hunting. Today, in

'ĀLALUKA **HALEY KAILIEHU**

SPYHOP IN KACHEMAK BAY **EMMA LUCK**

Spyhopping calf AD58 Mansfield (born 2018) with their uncle, AD27 Angiak, in Kachemak Bay, Alaska, 2018.

Kinship

'Cúagilákv Jess Housty

I. SLOW ROLLS IN THE FOG

ONCE WHEN I WAS A LITTLE GIRL I was in a skiff with my father. (This sentence is how all my best childhood stories begin.) This particular time, we were travelling from the village out to camp. It was spring, and the fog was so thick that we were travelling by instinct and memory. The vessel reminded me of a piece of driftwood: curved, light and somehow a little impermanent. I always sat perched high when we travelled in that boat, nestled on top of our gear, my hip to the gunwale so I could lean over and stare into the ocean.

As we puttered slowly down the channel,[1] a pod of orcas appeared. It was as though they'd manifested out of the dense fog, and although they overtook us quickly, their pace seemed to slow to match their curiosity. They surfaced and dove too quickly to count them all; it was orcas all the way down. They performed lazy rolls, the calves clumsy as they practised their spyhopping. Occasionally an adult would breach—with the elegance of a salmon and the enormous power of rolling thunder.

Their clicks and cries made the skiff shake, and their vocalizations vibrated up into my bones. The hull of the boat was the most fragile of liminal spaces dividing me from the whales, and the closeness made me feel a sense of deep safety—like the ocean was a womb and they were the pulse of my mother, beating all around me.

They paced us for awhile, the females and their calves closest to the boat and the rest of the pod radiating outward. The dorsal fins that cut the surface were dark against the backdrop of the ocean, and darker against the fog. And there we were, my father and I, cupped in the curve of our little skiff with the barrier between ocean and sky dissolving all around us.

Gradually, the pod carried on ahead of us. And the last we saw was a magnificent bull whose massive head plowed straight toward our boat, turning into a slow dive so close to us that the top of his dorsal fin was within arm's reach just before he disappeared beneath the hull.

I thought I would feel bereft in that moment; instead I felt full. And to this day, nearly three decades later, that moment is what slips into my mind when I think of the definition of prayer.

II. KINGDOM UNDER THE SEA

IN THE HAÍⱢZAQV (HEILTSUK)[2] WAY of knowing the world, there is a kingdom under the surface of the ocean that is as complex and organized as our society above the surface. The chief of this kingdom is a figure called Qvúmúgva. He is at the centre of a system of knowledge, laws, stories and governance that provides structure to the relationships between the species that form a community in the ocean; his authority also shapes how we relate to the constituents of the kingdom under the sea.

To accept Qvúmúgva's authority is to reject the colonial concept of human supremacy over the natural world, particu-

larly the ocean. Through the respect he commands, he reminds us that when we are in and on the ocean, the locus of power rests within his hierarchy—not ours. The oral history gifted to us down the generations from our ancestors teaches that the híx̌ʔínúx̌v, the orca, accompanies Qvúmúgva's house as he moves throughout his kingdom. The híx̌ʔínúx̌v is a signifier of Qvúmúgva's presence and authority, a herald that can move between worlds and communicate both above and below the ocean's surface.

In our relationship to the ocean, Qvúmúgva humbles us. He reminds us that a power greater than us is at play. And the híx̌ʔínúx̌v that travels with him, making his presence and power known, is a visual reminder of that call to be humble. Are you capable of feeling small without feeling threatened? How does your ego concede to proofs of nature's supremacy? When an apex predator and awe-striking being like a híx̌ʔínúx̌v spyhops or rolls slowly beside your boat, what do you feel when you meet its eye?

If we can put our instinctive anthropocentrism aside and accept what Qvúmúgva and his attendants represent—a system of undersea laws and governance in a marine society that operates independently of us— we can begin to understand that the ocean is not some *mare nullius* where we can exercise our sense of human entitlement.

ORCAS AND CERTAIN OTHER CETACEANS HAVE BEEN OBSERVED IN THIS SORT OF VIGIL FOR THEIR DEAD BEFORE, BUT THE LENGTH OF TIME AND THE PHYSICAL DISTANCE THAT THIS MOTHER CARRIED HER DEAD CALF IS NEW TO OUR HUMAN FRAME OF REFERENCE.

How does our behaviour change when the ocean is a sovereign space? When there is an authority figure, like Qvúmúgva, who sets a bar of accountability and respectful relations? When the beings who are citizens of that Nation are our kin?

Moving between worlds, the hĺx̌ʔínúx̌v is a reminder from Qvúmúgva to humble ourselves—a messenger who carries teachings of humility. If we have the capacity for humility, we have the capacity for respect and empathy. If we can embody that triad of teachings, maybe we can become the kind of relations that the hĺx̌ʔínúx̌v and other denizens of Qvúmúgva's kingdom deserve.

III. MOTHERHOOD AND GRIEF

LIKE MANY OTHERS, I watched with an ache in my heart in 2018 when Tahlequah, an orca in the Southern Resident J pod, nudged her dead calf to the ocean's surface for 17 days in what appeared to be a ritual of mourning.

Orcas and certain other cetaceans have been observed in this sort of vigil for their dead before, but the length of time and the physical distance that this mother carried her dead calf is new to our human frame of reference. It was widely reported as a "sad spectacle"—a phrase that implies a passivity in us, mere spectators. But I believe that grief was meant to be active—to be participatory.

Grief is ceremony. It can have elements that are both private and public, but when it is enacted in a public way, as Tahlequah's was, we can't be simple spectators. We need to be witnesses.

In Haíɫzaqv culture, to be a witness is a deep responsibility. It obligates you to be an archive embodied, ready to recall the events and the ceremonies you have witnessed and the business that has been conducted before you when the record of your testimony is required. In the context of a potlatch or a feast, the hospitality shown to you by the host and the gifts that you receive are how you are paid in advance for the testimony you may some day be called upon to provide. Memory is part of reciprocity.

In the context of Tahlequah's mourning, bearing witness is how we must reciprocate the ocean's generosity, the feasts it has provided us, the gifts it has given us.

COASTAL GIANT **NOELLE JONES**

Like orca pods, Haíɫzaqv society is gathered around matriarchs. We trace our ties through our mothers, our lifegivers. And inextricably linked to the ritual of birth is the ritual of death. While our matriarchs bring future generations into being through the ceremony of birth, they also perform many of the ceremonies that guide us through death and loss; these ceremonies honour the departed, but they also teach us, those who are still alive, a new way of being in the wake of death.

I don't know why Tahlequah's calf died. I can recite the pressures that bear down on the ocean, on orcas in general, on Tahlequah's pod in particular. I carry that anxiety in my bones like ocean salt etching into my marrow. Dwindling food sources. Chemical and noise pollution. The lingering intergenerational impacts of all the live captures in decades past. The hazards of shipping oil. The low howl of climate change. My empathy overwhelms me at times because what I see in our ocean relatives so closely parallels what I see in my own community; we've also felt starvation and contamination. We've also heard our languages drowned out by white noise and felt the intergenerational trauma of fractured families. We've also calculated what we stand to lose to an oil spill and stared down the uncertain future of a wildly shifting climate.

As a Haíɫzaqv mother, I am conscious every day that I owe my existence to the resilience of my ancestors through every generation from the time of creation to the day of my birth. My existence is a testament to their survival. And I feel a fierce urge to be part of the swell of resurgence for our people, to bring my Haíɫzaqv babies into the world, to be a good future ancestor. I want to be one little abalone button in the metaphorical ceremonial blanket that represents my matrilineal line back to our creation story. I want that blanket to be heavy with the weight and the richness of many generations to come after me.

I'm sure Tahlequah also feels that same imperative to survive, that generative force deep within her, that need to manifest a future where her genetic memory and intergenerational wisdom can carry on. I cannot imagine the deep grief of losing your offspring. If that mourning was an ocean, I'm not sure I could even imagine standing at its shore. But when I watched the footage of her nosing her dead calf to the ocean's surface, I felt her pain—in my head, my heart, my womb.

And when I watched her pod take turns lifting that calf up so she could rest as she completed her sacred work, Tahlequah reminded me that we do not move through grief and uncertainty alone. We do it with our community bearing witness. And our community endures.

THE WAY WESTERN SOCIETY INTERACTS WITH THE WORLD IS OFTEN ROOTED IN DISCONNECTION, IN DISSOCIATION. WE THINK WE ARE ARCHITECTS OF THE ORDER OF THE WORLD, THAT OUR NEEDS ARE THE HIGHER NEEDS.

That Tahlequah lingered so long over her ritual of mourning should prompt us to ask ourselves whether we received her teachings and internalized what it was we witnessed. Did we respond with the care, attention and memory that her persistent grief called for? After all, we may be called upon someday to affirm the record on the ceremonies that Tahlequah performed. We are her oral historians. We are her chroniclers. What story did you write on your heart when you watched her?

IV. BUILDING COMMUNITY

I HAVE IMMENSE PRIVILEGE in my proximity to the ocean, to orcas and other beings, to the teachings they offer. And the framework of Haiłzaqv laws, principles, and values that informs my worldview helps me to locate myself within cycles and systems; from birth, I've been surrounded by people who model the difference between spectators and witnesses—the responsibilities of kinship. But if we want

to create the conditions for orcas and all ocean relatives to survive and to thrive, all of us—no matter whether our experience is direct or indirect—need to forge a connection.

The way western society interacts with the world is often rooted in disconnection, in dissociation. We think we are architects of the order of the world, that our needs are the higher needs. This kind of thinking is so firmly embedded in my broader social context, and when it creeps into my thinking I have to remind myself: think like an ancestor. If disconnection is the root cause of what has made our world, and the orcas' world, so precarious—the antidote is connection. Building connection is building community.

As I layer all these stories together—my own encounters with orcas, my Haiłzaqv ancestral teachings, the mourning rituals of Tahlequah—what resonates in my body, like whale song rising up through the hull of my father's skiff, is the belief that community building is the most important work before us. When we practice reciprocity, we spend our lives in service of our community, and we trust that our community's acts of service will lift us up as well. We become accountable to one another—interdependent.

We need to be part of the pod. We need to be the companions who shoulder Tahlequah's burden for awhile so she can rest in her grief and regain her strength. We need to be the collective that nourishes and protects all its constituent parts according to their needs. The planet needs us to be connected. The ocean needs us to be connected. The orcas need us to be connected. And through that sense of deep connection, we can build the trust that will help us bring the fullest of our capacity, creativity and compassion to addressing the complex and systemic challenges our world faces today.

The Haíłzaqv are an oceangoing people. My sense of connection to our waterways and our ocean kin is strong. Maybe you live in the mountains or the prairies. Maybe you live in the dense, urban environment of a major city. Maybe you're unsure of how to forge the kind of connection that will build community between you and a pod of orcas. But it's not an impossible task.

When I think about that spring morning in my childhood, and the black fins cutting through ocean and fog, I think about prayer. I feel humbleness, gratitude and a sense of safety. I feel community. I feel home. What makes you feel those things?

Sometimes building community is about exercising vulnerability and allowing yourself to be cared for. Sometimes it's about power and wielding it in a way that it shelters your kin. As you reflect on your own life, ask yourself where your strongest sense of connection is rooted. Find the analogue in your life that parallels what the hí x̌ʔínúx̌v, what the orca, is to me. Wear that sense of connection boldly, like a gleaming white saddle patch. Find your pod. And in the sense of purpose and resilience that community responsibility generates, know that you have power. ⟿

Notes

1 Seaforth Channel, near the site of the *Nathan E. Stewart* diesel spill of 2016.

2 The main Haíłzaqv (Heiltsuk) community is Bella Bella, a village on Campbell Island on British Columbia's central coast.

Kakaw ìn

Kā'ānni Valeen Jules

I believe in sovereignty
I believe in self-determination
I believe in safety
I believe in the Salish Sea
I believe in you
I believe in me
I believe in everything and everyone
we're meant to be

I believe in birth
I believe in Mother Earth
I believe in the timing of the tides
when they retreat and when they return

I believe in burdens
I believe in purpose
I believe you're worth it
Say it over and over
until you believe it too
Just stay true to you
Take back the land
Withstand the pain
Regain our rights
Remain the same
Sacred, cherished
Don't let them perish

I believe in life
I believe in the darkness
I believe in rest
I believe in the harvest
I believe in hydration
I believe in our nations

I believe in land reclamation
I believe in water liberation
Every *kakaw ìn* (orca), every waterway
I believe in you every day

T'aq'aks Haawiłmis

TRANSLATED **into nuučaanuł** BY **Čiisma Patti Frank** and **Tupaat Julia Lucas**

t'aq'aks hą ʔakmis
t'aq'aks ƛułʕup
t'aq'aks ʕuuc'uct
t'aq'aks suwa'
hišʔałks t'aaak
t'aq'aks qwaaniš qwaaʔin
t'aq'aks hinuł
t'aq'aks maanuł

t'aq'aks haayiičałquu
ʔuhį š muułšaaʔaƛquu
t'aq'aks hiiwatmis
t'aq'aks qwaačukʔii

t'aq'aks qwaanumšuk
ʔiihįrʔaƛqukʔiiʔiihąt
qwiyuuʔaƛquk
t'aqakšiƛ
qwaʔsasa t'aakuukłi
huuʔiip nišma
wiksaa y'ay'ačup
huuʔiisuk
qwiqwinkin
wikšuk qwisʕhį nšiƛ
ʔaasusmupʕapkin
wikpaawłšiƛ

t'aq'aks kaƛʕk
t'aq'aks tuumaƛk
t'aq'aks pusʔaatu
t'aq'aks cišƛhaaʔumʔstyup
t'aq'aks ƛuštʕiiʕa
t'aq'aks Matmas yk kin

t'aq'aks huuʔip nisma
t'aq'aks čaʔakʕaqkin
hišił kaakaawin
hišił caʔuk
taqaksiš suwa hišyuuya ➳

ORCA FUTURESCAPE **SANTIAGO X**

ORCINUS ORCA SKAANAA

Michael Nicoll Yahgulanaas

THIS PAINTING BY HYBRID ARTIST MICHAEL NICOLL YAHGULANAAS, reproduced in full inside your book's dust jacket, was commissioned for the Royal BC Museum's 2020 exhibition *Orcas: Our Shared Future*. Its structure, defined by curving blue formlines, reflects designs associated with the artist's home community in Haida Gwaii and depicts the face of the wealthy Lord of the Sea. Within that framework are scenes of human-orca interactions across time, space and cultures, portrayed in the artist's unique Haida Manga style.

Carried to the undersea village of the killer whales

This narrative tells of a young woman carried away by SKAAnaa, the orca, to marry the 7laanaas Auu (town Mother) of the undersea village. But before she can be finned and thereby transformed into a SKAAnaa, she is rescued by Nanasimget and friends and returns to her Haida village.

Ancestral peoples

Indigenous societies around the world have longstanding, complex relationships with orcas. These ancestral peoples are shown here as witnesses from the past. These memories and inherited values watch our contemporary activities and relationships with orcas, and—let's hope—those of our descendants.

Face of the orca

Ocean pollution impacts the SKAAnaa home. Here liquid drains from a pipe. The liquid represents bitumen and tar sands infrastructure and the liquid waste flowing into ocean waters. The liquid delineates the face of the ocean. The eyes are small orcas. The treatment of the undulating blue field is marked by small waves and ripples so that the entire framing device in the mural becomes the ocean.

Part of the family

For the Haida and other Indigenous peoples of the northeastern shores of the Pacific, orcas are part of an inclusive concept of family. Here a stylized figure wears a button blanket decorated with a Killer Whale crest design, signifying kinship. Enfolded by the button blanket, a contemporary woman wears a Naaxin headdress created by Lisa Hageman Yahgujanaas. The young woman is Mirella Nicoll of the Auu Gitins lineage. She reaches out to offer us a cedar bark hat that shelters us below the sea lion whiskers, which arise out of a swirl of rain clouds and winds.

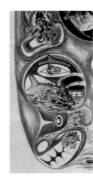

Once seen as monsters

As far back as Roman times, orcas were seen as sea monsters. Here a Haida Manga representation of a killer whale contrasts with an image of a fearsome orca, based on a drawing from an early European map, as imagined by mariners of the past.

Orca behind bars

The brutal capture and display of orcas in aquariums, where they were (and in some places still are) confined in small tanks and taught to perform tricks for audiences, was big business. Yet it was through observing orcas in captivity that attitudes began to change, as people came to realize the intelligence of orcas and the complexity of their society.

Haida connections

In Indigenous thought, orcas interact with, and are part of, the human world. A Double-finned Killer Whale is a crest of the Yahgulanaas lineage of the Haida. Bufflehead ducks are the killer whales' messengers, and sometimes a quick snack.

Threats to the oceans, threats to the orcas

Noise from ships' engines, rafts of garbage including plastics, industrial overfishing and the long assault on salmon that orcas depend on for food, global warming and environmental degradation: these human-made conditions impact the orcas' ocean homes and threaten the entire function of the world depicted in this Haida manga mural.

Shooting orcas

Fishermen saw salmon-eating orcas as threats to their livelihood and were encouraged to shoot them. Here an octopus, a species known for its intelligence, grasps the fish boat's gun and threatens to capsize the hunter ship.

Celebrating a birth

An orca swims past a kelp bed. A classic Haida design killer whale has surfaced in the mural to join in celebration of the latest baby orca.

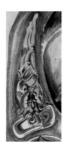

Noise pollution

A human figure squeezing out of the depths of the ocean frameline shrieks and roars into the ear of an orca.

An orca's assistance

A narrative of a trans-Pacific canoe journey is depicted here. A human couple was blown out to sea and travelled for a month, arriving on the shores of Asia, where they remained for five years. Their journey home, marked by guide birds, ends with the assistance of an orca that pulled them back to the Duu Guusd region of Haida Gwaii.

An orca family: J pod

J pod is a matriarchal family of Southern Resident orcas, each with distinctive physical characteristics (such as markings and fin shapes) that make them easy to identify and name. The orcas captured for aquariums mostly came from J pod; the scientific study of orcas began with them. Each orca here is shown with its personal identification number and displays some of its known and catalogued physical characteristics.

Northern Transients

Seals and other sea mammals are a major food of the Northern Transient orcas, whose home includes Haida Gwaii. This Northern Transient population appears more stable, while the numbers of the Southern Resident orcas such as J pod are rapidly declining.

Who's threatening whom?

Here a killer whale appears to threaten a ship, but an oil spill and acoustic assault from one of the many oil-powered ships that traverse the world's oceans would threaten the orcas' environment.

ARTISTS' STATEMENTS

Fanny Aïshaa
Joy of Coming Home
Acrylic, 40" x 30"

This painting is to celebrate our interdependency, connection and responsibility to salmon. It's a reminder of the gift of reciprocity we carry to protect salmon and healthy oceans. In order to see the Resident orca population thrive again, as numerous as they deserve to be, we must offer our sacrifices and gifts back to the salmon and ocean, who provide everything (for us) since time immemorial. This painting was intended to portray the threat orcas and salmon encounter every day through the noise from tankers, pathogens, pollution and fish farms placed through salmon migration routes. But instead, I decided to paint a dream I cherish of a quiet ocean, where whales can silently nurse their babies, where matrilineal systems and intergenerational power can shine through the Pacific waters, where chinook salmon can travel their stellar routes following the universe and complete the miracle they are. It's a painting to show the joy of a silent ocean without human interference, where orcas can share freely their family songs, language, and supernatural existence. When I paint salmon I share my gratitude and strength, and it reminds me it's time for us to give back to them, as they have given their life since prehistorical time to shape lands, forest, systems, cultures, everything. This painting is an ode to them, to feminine energy, matrilineality and the magical relationships that intertwine salmon and orcas. The little magic dot in the painting portrays this relationship and the magical power of echolocation.

Lauren Brevner and Nexw'Kalus-Xwalacktun James Harry
Pride
Oil, acrylic, washi and copper leaf on yellow cedar
20" x 20" x 3"

James Harry: Part of my job as an artist is to revitalize an art form that was almost lost. As we move into the future, our art will continue to evolve and grow, and my goal is to integrate our culture into the proudest segments of our society.

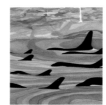

Jesse Campbell
Community
Acrylic and watercolour on birch panel, 24" x 24"

Everything in the Salish Sea is connected in one great circle. From the orcas to the water to the land and the trees. Everything is connected. In this piece I wanted to acknowledge the land, the water and the community that ties us together. The water is painted following the grain of the wood panel, and the whales are revealed through the shape of the grain. The shore and the trees are painted from the lines of the grain as well to acknowledge their connection within the circle.

Rande Cook
Peace Treaty
Carved cedar

To truly understand the art of the northwest coast you must first understand how close our relationship is with the land, the ocean and all that lives. Since our earliest beginnings as the first peoples, our origin stories grew from tales on the land after the great flood subsided. It's our duty as the people of the land to live in harmony with the many other species and animals of Mother Earth.

This hand-carved cedar sculpture is the face of the boy who first met the killer whale, abstractly mirrored in the killer whale's tail. Our art forms always merge entities between human and animal showing the energies are that of the same. From the oceans to the land, we are all one, we believe. In early times it was said the orcas had beached themselves and transformed into wolves; the wolves also carry the same family values as the orca; these family values and societal structures gave way to us as Indigenous peoples within our governance systems. It was the early treaty between humans and the killer whales that also helped with the understanding of the whole sea kingdom. The killer whales gave protection to humans and helped with gathering food. And it's said today that it's the spirit of the killer whale that can sense death and will carry the human spirit off through the thin veil into the heavens and beyond.

This sculpture is my connection to the orcas, my way of saying thank you, I respect you, and will honour the treaty our people shared from our earliest times.

Andy Everson
Connection (cover)
and *Protection*

For the Kwakwa̱ka'wakw, killer whales are seen as our relatives. In my family, the maxinux is the main crest from my grandfather. As long as we treat them with respect, they will respond in kind. We used to travel great distances by carved dugout canoe and would often be greeted by great plumes of misty air as the orcas would breach nearby. As one of the more powerful creatures in the sea, a killer whale could easily lift a canoe and all of its occupants to deposit them into the frigid ocean. They didn't. They would talk to us, and we would talk back in mutual admiration and respect. As with humans, orcas will most often live together in groups; they rely on each others' protection and companionship. Also similar to people, there is nothing stronger than the maternal bond between mother and calf. For two years, a calf will breast feed and bond with its mother. For 13 more years, it will mature while playing and exploring under its mother's watchful eye. It will feel a true sense of protection. In recent times, some of us have lost our sense of respect for these whales. We will watch and admire them, while doing little to stop the destruction of their habitat. Many local populations are in danger. It is up to us to provide more protection for the maxinux.

Christian Geissler
Small Craft Warning
Acrylic on canvas, 36" x 48"

As a biologist and lover of nature I am always fascinated by the connections within natural ecosystems. Everything is connected. That which is seen and unseen in the air, the soil and the water. Through my art I wish to bridge the gap between humans and nature and create the same appreciation and wonder. I attempt to create a vibrant and hyper-surreal world that shows those ecological connections of the west coast of British Columbia.

My process is to use strong colours and lines evoking a sense of temperature and movement in my work. I create using acrylics layered upon layers without shading, to where the final piece appears to be blended when viewed as a whole, but any small piece up close reveals layers of contoured lines. For subject matter I usually rely on the endless images of wildlife and seascapes that I have collected in my mind from a lifetime of living and working on the ocean around Vancouver Island.

Noelle Jones
Coastal Giant

Since moving to British Columbia four years ago, I have had the privilege of exploring its beautiful unceded lands and learning about the critical threats they continually face. From pipelines to fractured salmon populations to the issue of dramatically low numbers of the Salish Sea orcas and beyond, I now consistently strive to contribute to address conservation issues in small ways wherever I can. While I am fortunate that my job and community allows me to continually learn and take part in these causes, I felt that I could perhaps lend my own personal offering through illustration.

A month ago, an orca came to me in a dream, and I felt strongly that I needed to acknowledge through creative means the best I could. As the orca is so central to coastal life and Indigenous culture and history, I feel incredibly honoured to be a part of a project focused on the celebration and protection of this magnificent animal.

Haley Kailiehu
'Ālaluka
Digital rendering, 8" x 10"

Art is the language of the people, the language of the community. It is most powerful as a tool for interpreting and representing the world we live in. Art can help us develop close relationships with 'āina and make us able to gather these strengths and supports for navigating modern pathways.

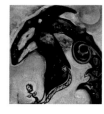

Eric Mazimpaka
A Fine Balance

A delicate dance occurs in mother nature. Only understood by creatures who quietly dance back.

Paul Morstad
Interstellar Sea Lions
Watercolour, 22" x 30"

In the hinterland between tangled wilderness and tidy civilization is where I place the semi-fictitious narrative fragments which make up my drawings and paintings. These narratives are chronicles of the liminal and construct a loose scaffolding of a realm that is both aqueous and terrestrial. This world is built on history and geography, zoology and mythology, musicology and astronomy, rumours, lies, hyperbole and folklore.

Sometimes based on legend, a dream or just a remnant of something overheard, my compositions are maps which chart that threshold when you are just about to fall asleep, when unrecognizable yet familiar voices call out to you and your body feels paralyzed. It is a type of purgatory inhabited by wandering nomads, tricky hobos, long-dead composers, defunct societies, distant relatives, extinct animals, forgotten deities and mythical beasts, who all reluctantly coexist somewhere between discord and euphony.

My thematic explorations touch on migration, encroachment, ecological decay, extirpation and extinction. The media I use range from oil on panel to watercolour, pen and ink, and intaglio printmaking processes. I also make short animated films with similar themes.

Ray Troll
The Whale Family Tree
Pen and ink with digital colour, 16" x 19"

Moving to Alaska in 1983 exposed me to the forces of the natural world, changed my life, and transformed my art. Living with deep woods on one side and the deep ocean on the other is magical for me and informs my art like no other influence.

Over the years my curiosities have led me to befriend scientists, writers and musicians. I came to realize that scientific inquiry and artistic inquiry overlap beautifully, as both disciplines seek to know the world in complex and elegant ways. The cross currents between art, science, music and literature are the waters in which I prefer to swim.

Chris von Szombathy
Orca Sonar

What we're looking for is out there, even if it's distant. We can see farther than we think if we start by closing our eyes.

Santiago X
Orca Futurescape
Virtual reality capture
14" x 24"

Indigenous Futurism is now. The trajectory of my practice is an exploration of the human interface between our built environment, history, technology, our own self-relevance, and how we navigate this relationship to construct our notions of order, in an infinite world of chaos. I make to transform the threshold where art becomes an artifact, back to art again. As an Indigenous Futurist, I believe that art can transcend representation and become something sacred that embodies life itself, through a multiplicity of being. My work directly engages the notions of a post-human world, but actualizes to activate the possibility of our own prosperity by painting our self-constructed limitations and deconstructing them.

CONTRIBUTORS

Fanny Aïshaa is a self-taught nomadic painter, adopted and raised through different villages in the boreal forest in "Quebec," where she developed a strong connection with biodiversity. Her family originates from the coastal peninsula of Gaspésie and from Morocco. In the streets of Brazil, she learned the power of murals to revitalize and reclaim spaces, voices, stories and diaspora identities. Since then, she has travelled from coast to coast to share her passion for painting collective murals with communities and youth-led projects.

Ken Balcomb obtained his bachelor's degree in zoology in 1963 from the University of California, Davis, and soon after was employed by the US government as a field biologist GS5-7. As a graduate student, Ken conducted humpback whale research in the North Atlantic with colleague Dr. Steve Katona and taught marine biology aboard RV *Regina Maris*. Ken is a pioneer in photo-identification of cetaceans. He founded the non-profit Center for Whale Research in 1985 and remains the principal investigator for Orca Survey. Ken is devoting his remaining life to saving the Southern Residents and the chinook salmon they depend upon.

'Láanaas Sdang Adam Bell, 1902–1987, was the hereditary chief of the Gaw Yahgu 'Láanaas, one of the clans of the Massett Haida people or Gaw Xaadee of Haida Gwaii. He was the last traditionally trained storyteller and orator in Massett. He took his chieftainship during a potlatch in about 1913, during the height of the Canadian government's anti-potlatch legislation, also taking the name Xiláa from his maternal great-uncle. From 1980 to 1987 he recorded a number of epic Haida clan stories with Marianne Boelscher (Ignace) and Lawrence Bell. One of these is The Two Brothers at Tiiaan, presented in this volume.

HIGáawangdlii Skilaa Lawrence Bell of the Sdast'aas Eagle clan in Haida Gwaii is a fluent speaker of Xaad Kil, the Massett Dialect of the Haida language. As the son of the late 'Láanaas Sdang Adam Bell and T'aaw Guud Nang Kaas Ruth Bell, he was one of the last people raised in a fully Haida-speaking home. He works with Dr. Marianne Ignace on translating and transcribing recordings of 'Láanaas Sdang and other Haida elders made in the 1970s and 1980s. In recent years he has also worked with learners of Xaad Kil to produce digital media materials for Xaad Kil, develop curricular resources and revive the ancient art of storytelling in the language, connecting knowledge of gyáahlan.gee (stories) to knowledge of places, past people and their activities.

April Bencze's life centres on the resilience, beauty and limitless generosity of salmon. She dedicates her time to creative wildlife conservation work, visual storytelling and collaborative projects. She is committed to the well-being of coastal ecosystems and communities that she lives in and relies on. April was raised on Ligwilda'xw land near the Campbell River, and she currently lives and works in the unceded territories of the Musg̱amag̱w Dzawada̱'enux̱w Nations on Gilford Island. She works on salmon enumeration, streamkeeping initiatives and a local bear research project, engaging with the land and water in the practices of photography, filmmaking and writing.

bill bissett thes pome is from my nu book b r e t h / th treez uv lunaria selektid rare n nu pomes n drawings 1957–2019 from talonbooks KILLER WHALE was first publishd in awake in th red desert talonbooks 1968 ium originalee from lunaria n was on th first childrns shuttul from ther lunaria had run out uv oxygen   erthlings ar a veree strange specees 2 figur iuv always lovd sound n vizual poetree n lyrik politikul n narrativ poetree as well as non-narrativ thers alwayze sew much mor we can dew with langwage as well as painting n drawing latest nu cd th ride with pete dako on bandcamp i work as well at peer support group th secret handshake wher my paintings ar shown

Martha Black was the curator of Indigenous collections at the Royal BC Museum from 1997 until her retirement at the end of 2019. Her PhD in art history (University of Victoria) and MA in interdisciplinary studies (York University) focused on Heiltsuk art. In retirement she continues her interest in Canadian art, and in museum collections and how they reflect and influence perceptions of Indigenous cultures.

Lauren Brevner was born and raised in Vancouver, British Columbia. She grew up in a mixed-heritage family rich with culture and inspiration. In 2009 she moved to Osaka, Japan, where she had the honour of apprenticing under renowned artist Sin Nakayamal. The composition of her paintings explores mixed media through the use of oil, acrylic and resin. This unique technical style is combined with a collage of Japanese chiyogami, yuzen and washi paper on wooden panels. Her influence originates from the stylistic elements of traditional Japanese art and culture. She aspires to reinvent the eloquent tradition of using gold and silver leaf in art.

GwaaG̱anad Diane Brown is an award-winning educator, healer and nanaay (grandmother). A language- and knowledge-holder of Ts'aahl Eagle clan of the Haida Nation, she has lived her whole life on the land and waters of Haida Gwaii, food gathering and learning and practising Haida medicine. She is a defender of the Earth and has always stood up for Haida Gwaii: in 1985, GwaaG̱anad was arrested trying to stop logging on Lyell Island. She is one of the founders of SHIP, the Skidegate Haida Immersion Program, now in its 21st year, and of the Skidegate Language Nest, which exposes mothers and babies to the Haida language.

Melanie Nagy / CTV News.

Jesse Campbell is an emerging visual artist with Métis, Scottish, Cree, English and German ancestry living on Lək̓ʷəŋən territory. Jesse is primarily a mural painter, a journey that started in 2010 with the guidance of Butch Dick and Darlene Gait of the Esquimalt and Songhees nations. The principal inspirations behind Jesse's work are story, history and interaction. Many of Jesse's murals have a historical component woven into them, whether personal or place-based. Jesse often uses "traditional" motifs to critique the contemporary.

Tavish Campbell's work brings conservation stories to light through underwater cinematography and photography. Engaged in commercial fishing from the age of 12 and in coastal conservation and environmental justice work from 15, Tavish grew up off-grid on the boat-access-only Sonora Island, off the west coast of Canada. Currently, he is focusing on the protection of the coast by revealing the complex stories of wild salmon, herring and old-growth forests. A commercial diver, maritime captain and wilderness guide, he can be found aboard his expedition vessel MV *Harlequin*, spouting fish love to anyone who will listen.

Jason M. Colby is professor of environmental and international history at the University of Victoria and the author of *Orca: How We Came to Know and Love the Ocean's Greatest Predator* (Oxford University Press, 2018). Although born in Victoria, he grew up in the Seattle area. During his high school and undergraduate years, he worked as a commercial fisherman in Alaska and on fish farms in Puget Sound. He earned his PhD from Cornell in 2005 and taught at the University of Texas at El Paso before coming to the University of Victoria in 2007.

Rande Cook, k'alapa is a Kwakwaka'wakw multimedia artist born in culture-rich Alert Bay. Cook grew up surrounded by the beauty of art and land, observing and discussing the traditional art forms of his Kwakwaka'wakw forefathers with his grandfather, Gus Matilpi. He has studied under several master craftsmen to learn traditional jewellery and carving techniques, including under master carver John Livingston. With strong teachings from his grandparents about culture and the sacred ceremonies of the Potlatch world, Cook became an accomplished singer and dancer, and learned the values that prepared him to be a strong leader for his people. He carries two chieftainships: the Hamatam/Seagull, and the Gigalgam from the ancient ancestor Kwanusila/Thunderbird.

Severn Cullis-Suzuki is an Earth Charter commissioner, host of an APTN TV series and a board member of the David Suzuki Foundation. At nine, Severn started the Environmental Children's Organization with friends, delivering a speech to the UN at twelve. She holds a BSc in biology from Yale and an MSc in ethnoecology from the University of Victoria. Twelve years ago Severn moved to her husband's community in the archipelago of Haida Gwaii and began to study X̱aayda kil (the Skidegate dialect of the Haida language) with elders. Today she is pursuing a PhD at the University of British Columbia with the goal of supporting the revitalization of the Haida language.

Andy Everson was born in Comox, BC, in 1972 and named Nagedzi after his grandfather, the late Chief Andy Frank of the K'ómoks First Nation. Andy has also had the honour of being seated with the 'Namgis Tsitsaɫ'walagame' name of Ḵwamxạlagalis I'nis. Influenced by his grandmother, he has always been driven to uphold the traditions of both the K'ómoks and Kwakwạka'wakw First Nations, pursuing opportunities to sing traditional songs and perform ceremonial dances at potlatches. Although he began drawing Northwest Coast art at an early age, it wasn't until 1990 that he started designing and painting blankets for use in potlatch dancing. He has tried to follow his Kwakwạka'wakw relatives in creating bold and unique representations that remain rooted in the traditions of his ancestors.

Gary Geddes has written and edited 50 books of poetry, fiction, drama, non-fiction, criticism, translation and anthologies and won a dozen national and international literary awards. His books include *Drink the Bitter Root* and *Medicine Unbundled: A Journey Through the Minefields of Indigenous Health Care*, *Falsework*, *Swimming Ginger*, *What Does a House Want?* and *The Resumption of Play*. He has a PhD from the University of Toronto and has taught at Concordia, Western Washington University and University of Missouri–St. Louis and has been writer-in-residence at the University of Alberta, UBC's Green College, Ottawa University and the Vancouver Public Library. He lives on Thetis Island with his wife, the novelist Ann Eriksson.

Christian Geissler grew up on the west coast of British Columbia, hiking, fishing, skiing, camping and doing whatever else you can think of doing outdoors. In 1996 he was accepted to the Visual Arts program at the University of Victoria, but soon moved into biology and graduated with a BSc. For most of his adult life he didn't pick up a paintbrush. After many years working as a biologist, consultant, adventure guide and expedition leader from the Arctic to the Antarctic, he finally picked up a paintbrush once again and instantly fell back in love with it.

Lorne Hammond has been a curator of history at the Royal BC Museum since 1997. In the exhibition *Orcas: Our Shared Future*, he is the curator responsible for popular culture and historical content (objects and images), and he works with academic experts, activists and aquarium staff. In 1997 he wrote posthumous biographical dictionary entries for orca activists Michael Bigg and Robin Morton, whose wedding he attended. He holds a PhD in history from the University of Ottawa and is an adjunct professor of the Department of History, University of Victoria.

© Lillie Louise Major, 2018, for Montecristo Magazine

Gavin Hanke is the curator of vertebrate zoology at the Royal BC Museum. He has described and named 10 new fossil fish species, works with Canada's Department of Fisheries and Oceans to document marine fish distributions, and is working on a series of papers detailing many new species records and species range extensions along the BC coast. Gavin also works with the BC Ministry of Environment to collect and monitor exotic vertebrates.

Nexw'Kalus-Xwalacktun James Harry's work stands on the foundation of the experience of growing up as a member of the Skwxwú7mesh Úxwumixw (Squamish Nation) and his affiliation with Coast Salish leaders. In his art he combines the use of modern tools, materials and techniques to integrate the traditional with the contemporary. He is committed to continuing the journey of self-discovery while studying and responding to the voice developed through his ancestors' way of creating. His artwork is attached to his own multifaceted identity, and also to a larger lineage of Indigenous artists, dancers, weavers and thinkers who have shaped and formed Indigenous culture and art up to this moment in time.

'Cúagilákv Jess Housty is a citizen of the Haíɫzaqv Nation. She works in service of community in both governance and grassroots capacities. She is an activist, a plant worker, and an advocate for land-based learning and healing. Jess lives in her homeland in Bella Bella with her husband and two sons.

Steve Huxter was born and raised in the coastal community of Powell River, BC. He is a former marine-mammal trainer, specializing in orcas, and he supervised the operations of the Victoria Marine Animal Rescue Centre for 10 years. Steve was part of the documentary film *Blackfish* and continues to be active in advocacy for orcas in captivity and those that live free. As an animal behaviourist, he has worked with thousands of companion animals and has also worked as a project manager in wildlife research. Currently, Steve is a member of the advisory group with the Whale Sanctuary Project and lives in Victoria, British Columbia.

Gulḵiihlgad Marianne Ignace is professor of linguistics and First Nations studies at Simon Fraser University and director of SFU's First Nations Languages Program and Research Centre. A resident of the Skeetchestn community in the Secwepemc Nation, she currently teaches and coordinates courses in Indigenous languages in Kamloops, Haida Gwaii and Yukon, and directs a SSHRC partnership grant focused on First Nations language documentation and revitalization. With Ron Ignace she was awarded the 2019 Governor General's Innovation Award, and she is currently completing two annotated and illustrated volumes of narratives in X̱aad Kil (Haida, with Lawrence Bell) and Secwepemctsin (Shuswap, with Ron Ignace). Among her many publications is *Secwepemc People, Land and Laws – Yeri7 re Stsq̓ey̓s-kucw*, a prize-winning epic journey through 10,000 years of Secwépemc history.

Noelle Jones is an artist born and raised in the Rockies of Alberta, now living on the west coast of British Columbia. Growing up playing outside gave Noelle a passion for everything wild, and now, as an adult, she finds true solace in the chaos and stillness of nature. It is this that inspires the majority of her work. She found art after an injury had shifted her life's trajectory away from her former athletic pursuits. Outside of illustrating, she is still an avid surfer and skier, and elements from both of these worlds are often present in her work.

Kāʻānni Valeen Jules is a queer former foster kid, former homeless youth and first-year college dropout from the nuučaanuł and kwakwa̱ka̱'wakw nations. Valeen keeps busy as a full-spectrum birth worker, radio producer, youth advisor, artist outreach worker, writer and facilitator throughout the West Coast. Valeen can be found delivering babies in the 'hood or getting tattoos on the airwaves during her "days off."

Jukka Jantunen is a Finnish-born, Yukon-based wildlife photographer and biologist, passionate about birds. Jukka works mostly on various population monitoring projects, together with the Yukon Bird Observatories, Environment Canada and Environment Yukon.

Haley Kailiehu was born and raised in the 'ili 'ina of Kukuipuka, a beautiful pu'uhonua in the ahupua'a of Kahakuloa, on the island of Maui. She graduated from the University of Hawai'i at Mānoa with a BA in art, with a focus in drawing and painting. As an artist and researcher she is currently interested and invested in creating community-centred and 'āina-rich experiences that allow the current and future generations of Kanaka 'Ōiwi to (re)learn and assert their kuleana, (re)establish connections to our mo'olelo (histories) and kūpuna (ancestors), and (re)affirm our rightful place in our homeland.

Mark Leiren-Young is the writer of the Royal BC Museum's *Orcas: Our Shared Future* exhibition. His best-selling book about Moby Doll, *The Killer Whale Who Changed the*

World, won the 2017 Science Writers and Communicators Book Award. He has three new books about orcas for younger readers: *Orcas Everywhere*, *Orcas of the Salish Sea* and *Big Whales, Small World*. Mark wrote and directed the award-winning documentary *The Hundred-Year-Old Whale* and is host of the *Skaana* podcast. When he's not writing about whales, Mark is one of Canada's top comedy writers. In 2009 he won the Leacock Medal for Humour for his memoir, *Never Shoot a Stampede Queen*.

Jack Lohman, CBE, is the chief executive officer of the Royal BC Museum. Before joining the Royal BC Museum, he was the director of the Museum of London and CEO of Iziko Museums of Cape Town, South Africa. He is president of the Canadian Museums Association, a board member and former chairman of the National Museum in Warsaw, Poland, and a member of the Executive Board of the Canadian Commission for UNESCO.

Emma Luck is a naturalist and educator who specializes in marine mammal science. Born and raised in Alaska, she holds a degree in marine biology from the University of Alaska Southeast and actively participates in killer whale research in south-central Alaska, focusing on the photo-identification of whales in Kachemak Bay.

Misty MacDuffee is a biologist and the director of the Wild Salmon Program for the Raincoast Conservation Foundation. She

has worked on salmon conservation and management for the past 15 years. The project she is most excited about now focuses on habitat conditions for juvenile chinook salmon in the Fraser River estuary. She also works to understand the implications of declining chinook abundance and fisheries management on Southern Resident killer whales. She sits as a representative to several Fisheries and Oceans Canada working groups, including the Salmon Integrated Harvest Planning Committee, the Southern BC chinook Strategic Planning Initiative, and the Stakeholder Advisory Group on Southern Resident killer whales.

Eric Mazimpaka was born in 1987 in Nairobi, Kenya. At present, he resides and works in Vancouver, Canada. His artwork interfaces with the rich history of East African art by assimilating its styles and mediums. Mazimpaka casts, cuts, colours and amalgamates the works of classical and renaissance painters with a contemporary African pulse, creating ceremonious themes composed of bright colours aligned with newer tales of Afrofuturism.

Paul Morstad is an avid bird watcher, musician and traveller. His interests in zoology, geography, history, literature and exploration have led him on many journeys, and he has shown his work in Montreal, Paris, Toronto, Seattle, Vancouver, Miami and Portland, Oregon. Born and raised in the western provinces, Paul studied at Emily Carr Institute of Art and De-

sign before moving east to Montreal to work for the National Film Board of Canada, where he directed short, hand-drawn animated films. His longing for the Pacific Rim brought him back west to East Vancouver, where he now lives and works. When not painting and drawing, Paul can be found on his bike looking for birds or hanging out with his wife and daughter.

Alex Morton decided as a girl to follow in the footsteps of Dr. Jane Goodall, and when she followed whales into Musgamagw territory in 1984, she realized this was the place she would spend her life. The first 10 years were full of wonder as she began investigating what whales say, what matters to them and who they are. But she was also faced with the reality that human activity was severing the flow of energy that keeps our world alive. Alexandra published scientific papers, went to court to uphold the laws of Canada, engaged in activism and stepped into the public arena. Today, she continues her work from her cabin by the sea with her dog, Arrow.

Adrien Mullin was born and raised on Vancouver Island, growing up between the Tla-o-quiaht, nuučaanuɫ, Kʼómoks and Dzawa̱da'enux̱w territories. He is the program director and community outreach liaison for Nimmo Bay Wilderness Resort, where he has worked as a wilderness guide and manager for the past five years. He was also the project lead and developer for Sea to Cedar's Coastal Carnivores project. The focus of his work has been creating education and mentorship programs for youth to connect with environmental and cultural stewardship. Passionate about leveraging tourism for stewardship over community and place, Adrien approaches photography as a tool for connecting people to ecosystems and the creatures that dwell in them.

© Billie Woods

Briony Penn is an award-winning writer/naturalist, combining punchy media skills with research affiliations at the University of Victoria and an artistic eye for nature and landscape. She is best known as a newspaper and magazine columnist and illustrator, having published more than 500 columns on natural/cultural history in regional newspapers and magazines. She received the Western Magazine Award for Best Columnist and Feature Writer in Western Canada, won the Silver Environment Educator Award in the Canadian Environmental Awards and was nominated for best North American columnist in alternative weeklies. Briony has spent the last 30 years communicating her love and knowledge of the natural history of the Salish Sea.

BC Archives MS-2902

Quitting school for photography at 14, **Jim Ryan** (1920–1988) became a naval photographer. Settling in Victoria, he worked for the *Daily Colonist* newspaper until 1953. His freelance work appears in *Life*, the *Vancouver Sun*, *The Province*, and *Maclean's*. The newly found images in this volume cover Jim's work at Sealand of the Pacific.

Nikki Sanchez is a Pipil/Maya and Irish/Scottish academic, Indigenous media maker and environmental educator. She holds a masters degree in Indigenous governance and is presently completing a PhD with a research

©Anita Cheung

focus on emerging visual media technology as it relates to Indigenous ontology. Previously, Nikki was the David Suzuki Foundation Queen of Green. For over a decade, Nikki has worked as a wilderness guide, Indigenous environmental educator and decolonial curriculum advisor.

Taylor Shedd holds a master of advanced studies in marine biodiversity and conservation from Scripps Institution of Oceanography, where his thesis research focused on the foraging behavior of Southern Resident Killer Whales. As the Soundwatch Program Coordinator at the Whale Museum in Friday Harbor, Washington, he is the principal investigator on National Marine Fisheries Service Research Permit 21114.

Paul Spong is the founder of OrcaLab, a land-based whale research station on Hanson Island, BC, and president of the non-profit Pacific Orca Society. He acquired a PhD in physiological psychology from the University of California, Los Angeles, in 1966. He began studying dolphins and orcas in 1967. His experiences led him into research with wild orcas and Greenpeace's involvement in the save-the-whales movement, which culminated in the moratorium on commercial whaling agreed to by the International Whaling Commission in 1982. In the 1980s, Paul returned to research at OrcaLab. Since then, with his wife, Helena Symonds, his work has focused on the long-term life history of the Northern Resident community of BC orcas.

David Suzuki is a scientist, broadcaster, author and co-founder of the David Suzuki Foundation. He is Companion to the Order of Canada and a recipient of UNESCO's Kalinga Prize for science, the United Nations Environment Program medal, the 2012 Inamori Ethics Prize and the 2009 Right Livelihood Award. Dr. Suzuki is professor emeritus at the University of British Columbia and holds 29 honorary degrees. He is familiar to television audiences as host of the CBC series *The Nature of Things* and to radio audiences as the original host of *Quirks and Quarks*. His written work includes more than 55 books, 19 of them for children. Dr. Suzuki lives with his wife and family in Vancouver, British Columbia.

Tsaqwasupp Art Thompson's (1948–2003) ancestral roots are in both Coast Salish (Cowichan) and Nuu-Chah-Nulth (Ditidaht) Nations. Art spent most of his childhood in a residential school, away from both his family and cultural traditions. Just before his twelfth birthday he was initiated into the Tlu-Kwalla along side his siblings. This ancient custom connected Art to his cultural heritage, which influenced his decision to become an artist. In 1967, Art enrolled in the Commercial Art Program at Camosun College in Victoria. During this time he began to explore Nuu-Chah-Nulth style design. He is considered to be one of the greatest Nuu-Chah-Nulth artists of the 20th century.

Jared Towers's research mainly focuses on the conservation and ecology of killer whale populations in both hemispheres, but also includes various studies on the abundance, movements and behaviours of other large

cetacean species such as blue, fin, humpback, grey, minke and sperm whales. Jared directs various cetacean research and incident response initiatives for several government and non-governmental organizations in Canada and abroad. Jared is from Vancouver Island and lives in Alert Bay, "Home of the Killer Whale," on the territory of the 'Namgis people.

Ray Troll draws and paints images that migrate from his studio in Ketchikan, Alaska, into museums, books and magazines and onto T-shirts sold around the globe. Basing his offbeat images on the latest scientific discoveries, Ray brings a street-smart sensibility to the worlds of palaeontology and ichthyology. Ray earned a bachelor's degree from Bethany College in Lindsborg, Kansas, and an MFA in studio arts from Washington State University in 1981. In 2008 he was awarded an honorary doctorate in fine arts from the University of Alaska Southeast.

Chris von Szombathy is a visual artist, designer, and musician of Japanese-European heritage who lives and works in Vancouver, Canada. His work has been shown and published across the world. He works in a diverse range of analogue and digital media, and his bright, graphic style explores our personal economies of emotional excess and loss. He also runs RXVP, a creative and graphic design studio, and produces music as AAA/Yupzone.

Kyler Vos was born and raised on Sproat Lake, just outside of Port Alberni on Vancouver Island. Kyler, his wife, Jaymee, and son, Thatcher, now reside in Tofino, where Kyler bases his photography business, art gallery and print shop. After graduating from college in Vancouver, Kyler moved to the coast, chasing surf and wildlife with camera in hand. After years of documenting the unique surf scene on Vancouver Island, Kyler is now the editor and senior photographer of Canada's only surf magazine, *SBC Surf*. Kyler has also spent the past 10 years guiding wildlife and fishing charters around Clayoquot Sound and Haida Gwaii, where most of his wildlife and landscape photographs are taken.

Rebecca Wellard has been studying cetaceans for the past 15 years, working across various disciplines, including bioacoustics, population ecology, cognitive behaviour and applied conservation. She completed her PhD investigating the vocal repertoire, social structure and dietary preferences of Australian and Antarctic killer whales.

Matt Whelan is a freelance writer and photographer who feels blessed to spend so much of his time sailing and guiding the length of the BC coast and beyond!

Santiago X is a descendant of North American mound builders and stone carvers from the Marianas Islands. He received a master of fine arts in studio art and technology from the School of the Art Institute of Chicago, a master of architecture from the University of Southern California and bachelor's in environmental design from the University of Colorado. Santiago X is an enrolled member of the Coushatta Tribe of Louisiana (Koasati) and Indigenous Chamorro from the Island of Guam USA (Hacha'Maori). Currently Santiago X is reinvigorating Indigenous mound building via two public earthwork installations being constructed along the Chicago and Des Plaines Rivers in Chicago, Illinois.

Michael Nicoll Yahgulanaas is an award-winning visual contemporary artist, author and professional speaker. His work has been seen in public spaces, museums, galleries and private collections around the globe, including the British Museum, Metropolitan Museum of Art, Seattle Art Museum and Vancouver Art Gallery. Yahgulanaas's publications include national bestsellers *Flight of the Hummingbird* and *RED, a Haida Manga*. When not writing or producing art, Yahgulanaas pulls from his 20 years of political experience in the Council of the Haida Nation and travels the world speaking to businesses, institutions and communities about social justice, community building, communication and change management.

INDEX